MONNOW BRIDGE AND GATE

1777   Printed as the Act directs. For S. Hooper   S. Sparrow

MONNOW GATE AND BRIDGE, MONMOUTH.

THIS plate prefents the fouth afpect of Monnow Gate and Bridge, fo called from the river over which it is conftructed. Both are mentioned in Leland's Itinerary, and indeed have undoubted marks of antiquity, but neither hiftory nor tradition afford any lights refpecting the date of their erection. As a picturefque object they have long been noticed by the connoiffeurs.

THIS view was drawn anno 1775.

A copper engraving by Sparrow of Monnow Bridge published in 1777 for Grose's *Antiquities of England and Wales* after a 1775 water-colour sketch attributed to Francis Grose (1731–91).

MONNOW BRIDGE AND GATE

M.L.J. Rowlands

ALAN SUTTON

In Association with Monmouth Museum

To Julia

First published in the United Kingdom in 1994
Alan Sutton Publishing Limited
Phoenix Mill · Far Thrupp · Stroud · Gloucestershire
in association with Monmouth Museum

First published in the United States of America in 1994
Alan Sutton Publishing Inc · 83 Washington Street · Dover · NH 03820

British Library Cataloguing-in-Publication Data
A catalogue record for this book is available from the British Library

ISBN 0 7509 0415 1

Library of Congress Cataloging-in-Publication Data applied for

Cover illustrations:
Front: A steel engraving of Monnow Bridge and Gate by W. Deeble after
a drawing by Henry Gastineau dating from the early 1820s.
Back: Monnow Bridge viewed from the north in December 1985.

Typeset in 9/11 Palatino.
Typesetting and origination by
Alan Sutton Publishing Limited.
Printed in Great Britain by
Redwood Books, Trowbridge, Wiltshire

Contents

Preface

Monnow Bridge and Gate, at Monmouth, Gwent, is a monument that has become a unique remnant of its class in Britain. It is the sole medieval fortified river bridge at which the gate tower stands actually upon the bridge.

The present stone Monnow Bridge was erected late in the 1200s over the remains of a mid-twelfth-century wooden bridge. The tower was added some thirty years later. At first the bridge was only slightly wider than the present road archway. The gate had a heavy wood and iron portcullis in front of the main doors. Other defensive features included arrow loops, machicolation, and a castellated parapet.

Over its seven hundred year history Monnow Gate has served several purposes other than defence. In the early 1700s the gate was converted to a house in which a porter lived. The building was heightened, an attic floor was created, and an extension hanging over the river was added facing what later became the cattle market.

Not until the nineteenth century was the tower pierced for pedestrian passageways. In the latter half of the 1800s the tower was used as a store-room until in 1900 the ninth Duke of Beaufort presented the gate to Monmouthshire County Council.

Until the twentieth century any building works at the bridge were usually carried out to redress the decay accompanying antiquity. But, since 1900, the steady increase in motorized traffic has greatly increased the frequency of repair works. Erection of a new bridge and closure of old Monnow Bridge to motorized traffic have been suggested, considered, and postponed on numerous occasions since the 1920s.

Despite attraction as a curiosity and as a microcosm of medieval defensive building, there has not been any appreciable interpretative display about the monument on site, and no broad written guide or history has been available. Most visitors only experience a cursory examination of the exterior in conjunction with a brief and vague gazeteer entry. Now, when closure to traffic and more ready access to the tower are within sight, this book is written in an effort to explain the building's design, the significance of its features, and to outline what is known of its use and role over the past seven hundred years.

A description and a history are the two main sections of this book, supported by explanatory sections. An account of the history of the bridge and gate is followed by a description, then by appendices containing document transcripts. Technical terms are avoided where possible in the text. However, a glossary is added. Historical information here is based upon original written sources or contemporary published works. Superscript numbers placed in the text refer to the notes, which contain references to these information sources and further explanation of points discussed in the text. Published sources are referenced by the author's surname and publication date (e.g. Evans 1987) and these are listed in the references section. Acknowledgements form the conclusion.

At the time of writing, the structure is still very much in use, with hundreds of pedestrians and vehicles crossing the bridge every day. It is still subject to change, both purposeful structural changes (like the modifications as part of Monmouth's recent flood alleviation scheme) and repairs to redress the decay of time and buffeting from motorized vehicles. If circumstances warrant, then this guide may appear in a revised edition in the future. Comments and information from readers are welcome, and these should be addressed to the author care of the publisher.

Bridge over the Monnow, Monmouth, a water-colour drawing dated 1831 by T.E. Rosenberg.

History

Despite the current fame of Monnow Bridge, in its early years it was an ordinary structure of a type that was not at all unusual. For a great number of gates, bridges, and castles across Britain significant records survive referring to their early history. These include letters, bills, orders, and journals. But, regrettably, Monnow Bridge is one of the multitude of surviving monuments whose early history is barely recorded in extant records. No direct written evidence exists dating from the first building of either the bridge or the tower gate. Thus, until any as yet unknown records are discovered, this account must rely chiefly upon evidence within the structure itself, and evidence suggested by relevant events in Monmouth. It is not until several centuries after the structure was built that significant references to it appear in official borough documents. Most detailed records date from only the mid-1700s.

Earlier Bridges
The confluence of two rivers afforded a defensible site promoting foundation of a town. Monmouth's siting with the Wye to the east and the Monnow to the west and south placed it in a protected position requiring man-made defence works only at the north to close the peninsula. The two rivers were not impenetrable barriers, but such obstacles could be a significant aid in protecting the community.

Recent excavations in and around Monmouth have revealed occupation of the site from long before the coming of the Normans. Monmouth was known in Roman times as Blestium, and considerable Roman artefacts, from the middle of the first century to late in the fourth, have been found at nearby Wonastow, at Overmonnow, and at several sites in the centre of Monmouth and down Monnow Street.[1] Due to its considerable depth, a bridge over the River Wye must have been erected during the settlement of Monmouth. But, since the Monnow was easily fordable at several points as it curved around the town, a Monnow Bridge may have developed later.

The first Monnow and Wye Bridges would have been timber structures with trestle-like piers possibly on piles driven in to the river bed. The old Wye Bridge at Chepstow survived in this form until the nineteenth century, and to this day there is a marvellous bridge of this sort at Whitney-on-Wye. Thus, long before the present stone Monnow Bridge was built, a wooden structure existed at or near the site.

The first reference to a timber Monnow Bridge is one of several that are indirect and disputed. A close roll made in the seventh year of Henry the Third's reign (1223) orders that John of Monmouth provide '*unu palefrm*' from the '*foresta de Dene*' for repair of the '*potis de Monem*'.[2] The term *Monem* is ambiguous since in the Latin of the time Monmouth and Monnow were rendered with several different spellings. *Monem* is usually taken to mean the town. This Monmouth Bridge could be a reference to what we call Monnow Bridge. But, considering the greater size of the Wye, and consequently the greater size of its bridge, unless there is contrary evidence it is almost certain that Monmouth Bridge would refer to Wye Bridge or its predecessor.

Just a decade later, the Battle of Monmouth on St Catherine's Day (25 November) 1233, during the rebellion of Richard the Marshal, brings another debatable early Monnow Bridge reference. Our accounts of this event come from *The Flowers of History* by Roger of Wendover, known as *Wendover's Chronicle*, and a revised version in Matthew Paris's *Greater Chronicle*.[3] Wendover died in 1236, so relatively his account was written very soon after the Battle. But, again the text is not clear enough to refer to any bridge unequivocally.

Wendover's Latin account describes the Battle fought on a field just outwith the town. The Marshal intended to subdue Monmouth, and with a hundred knights he proceeded to reconnoitre the castle and town with the intention of returning later accompanied by a strong force. But, spotted by Baldwin de Guisnes, to whom the King had entrusted Monmouth Castle, a force of one thousand men sallied forth from the castle to engage the Marshal's contingent. The ensuing battle took place either on Chippenham Mead or on Castle Field (Vauxhall). The Marshal's men acquitted themselves well against such an overwhelming force, and both leaders were seriously wounded. Forthwith the rest of the Marshal's army returned and soon put Baldwin's forces to flight. Baldwin's forces were thwarted in the vicinity of the castle by a broken-down bridge, causing many to drown with their horses and arms in their haste to escape. Few of those who sallied forth returned to the castle's safety.

Just as the battle could have occurred on two separate fields, the bridge described as near the castle could be Monnow Bridge or a predecessor of Tibb's Bridge, directly adjacent to the castle mound. If Baldwin's forces were attempting to escape to the castle, then it is unlikely that from Chippenham they would cross Monnow Bridge. Monmouth historian K.E. Kissack takes the view that Castle Field was the site and the bridge was Castle Bridge. Alternatively, E.N. Dew and J.G. Wood point out that in 1234 an order (close roll of 18 Henry III) was given for thirty oaks in the Forest of Dean to be delivered for the repair of the church of St Thomas the Martyr (i.e. St Thomas's Church, Overmonnow) which had burnt during the recent war. They infer that this destruction occurred when the adjacent timber Monnow Bridge was destroyed by fire during the Battle of Monmouth.[4]

Monnow Bridge in Stone

Based upon its design and construction, the stone Monnow Bridge could have been built at any point late in the thirteenth century or early in the fourteenth. No primary documents have come to light which specifically date its erection. In books dating back into the mid-nineteenth century, erection dates of 1262 or 1272 are repeated innumerable times, 1272 being the most popular choice. But this date appears to have become accepted simply due to its frequent repetition. Serious historians have declined to give a date simply because no original source is available which refers to building of the bridge. It is significant that authors naming 1272 have each given that date without indicating any primary source. Copying this information from other secondary sources is of course far simpler than fruitless searches through archives.

Until the nineteenth century, historians simply repeated Francis Grose's view of the gate and bridge that 'neither history nor tradition afford any lights respecting the date of their erection'. The earliest secondary historical source indicating 1272 as the date when Monnow Bridge was built appears to be a Victorian tome by William Beattie, his *Castles and Abbeys of England*. Beattie mentions the 'Saxon gateway' and states categorically that the bridge was erected by Edward I in 1272. There is no specific reference for this information, though Beattie does append a long list of obscure sources for this section on Raglan Castle and vicinity.[5]

With the assumption that Beattie or one of the other authors did in fact find evidence of the 1272 date, perhaps one should take 1272 as an hypothesis, to be retained until it is falsified.

Erection of Monnow Gate

The gatehouse atop Monnow Bridge forms a part of new town defences begun at the turn of the thirteenth century. Until that time Monmouth was without town walls. That is, it was not enclosed within masonry defensive walls. A castle had been founded by William Fitz Osbern by 1067–71 in the form of a motte and bailey on the site of the present castle remains. The castle was subsequently enlarged and rebuilt over several centuries until in 1673 Great Castle House was erected, where until 1647 a round tower had stood, built largely of ashlar plundered from the rest of the castle remains.[6]

The castle site was strong defensively on the north and west sides due to steep slopes down to the Monnow. On the east and south sides a ditch was cut crossed by a drawbridge half-way up the present Castle Hill Street. Outside of this inner bailey the Norman borough grew eastward towards the Wye. The town was enclosed along the north and south sides by the town ditch, which had a rampart and timber palisade on its inner side. A similar timber and earthwork defence was created around the suburb of Overmonnow. This Clawdd Du, the Black Dyke, continued as the perimeter of Overmonnow up to the 1930s, and it remains remarkably intact.[7] It is significant perhaps that Clawdd Du's tiny medieval bridge is aligned with Monnow Street and Monnow Bridge and may have been along an ancient route heading out towards Wonastow. Although Monmouth proper was enclosed in medieval times on high ground adjacent to the castle, as we have seen, Monnow Street and beyond formed a route long before the Normans arrived.

Town walls provided several benefits beyond the obvious asset of defensive protection. The protected area became more attractive as a trading centre. It allowed for the policing of people, and a monitor of the ingress and egress of travellers. Regulated crossing points at the gates allowed easier collection of tolls. And the gates themselves were often let or employed as gaols, lock-ups, or chapels. These town defences were most often financed by the populace through tolls. In the thirteenth century royal permission was required in order for town authorities to exact tolls. Thus, Henry of Lancaster, the King's nephew, petitioned Edward I to issue a murage grant in favour of Monmouth. The King assented. Edward authorized the 'Bailiffs and Honest Men of Monmouth' to take tolls for five years on certain goods brought to the town for sale so that the town defences could be replaced in stone. This authority was granted at Tonbridge in a patent roll entry made on 27 August 1297.[8] The document (Fig. 1 and Appendix A) is fascinating since it gives an indication of the foods and wares for sale in Monmouth at the time, but it is confusing since it is written in medieval Latin, a script packed with colloquialisms and English/Latin hybrid words.

It is following this 1297 murage grant that the Monmouth authorities were able to gather the wherewithal to build the medieval town walls and gates. Often in medieval town defences the importance of the gates was reflected in their

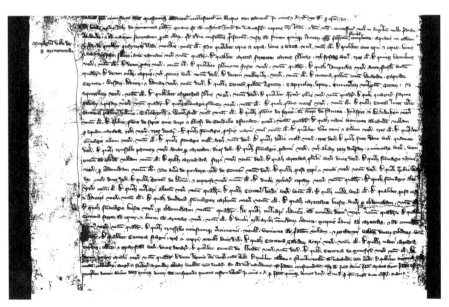

Fig. 1. Membrane six of a patent roll dated 1297 authorizing tolls to be taken in order for the Monmouth town defences to be rebuilt.

construction before the adjoining walls, and also in their careful design and provision of elaborate defensive features. Evidently the project at Monmouth was incomplete by 1315, or insufficient funding had been raised by the original grant, since the authority of 1297 was renewed on 1 June 1315 for a further three years.[9]

Lack of archaeological evidence prevents us from knowing how extensive these medieval defensive works were when they were complete, if ever. Gate towers were erected on Monnow Bridge, outside the then town proper, and at four or five sites around Monmouth – Monk's Gate (crossing Monk Street, near the Masonic Hall), Dixton Gate (across Dixton Road, now part of the Nag's Head Inn), Wye Gate (on Wye Bridge or in Wyebridge Street), St Stephen's Gate (almost at the top of Monnow Street), and, possibly, a West Gate with drawbridge over the ditch across Monnow Street near Nailer's Lane.[10]

The course of the stone town walls is not as certain at present. Their probable sites have yet to be extensively investigated, so we must rely partly upon contemporary written accounts. John Leland visited Monmouth during his tour of Wales between 1536 and 1539. In his words, '*Muro cingitur ea parte qua fluminibus non defenditur*', the town was enclosed along the north by a wall from river to river, from the Monnow to Monk's Gate and across to the Wye. Leland writes that extensive ruins of the wall remained along with a deep fosse. He lists the gates, '*Portae in muro 4^{or} videlicet monachica, orientalis, Vagensis, a Vaga sic dicta, Monensis, a Mona flu. quia super pontem per quem Mona transitur posita est*', being Monk's Gate, East (Dixton) Gate, Wye Gate, and Monnow Gate above the bridge that crosses the Monnow. William Camden, who toured in *c*.1574, confirms Leland's description. The fosse was a ditch crossing south of Glendower Street and St John Street. This continued beyond Monnow Street along Nailer's Lane to a position near Priory Mill; hence the siting of a drawbridge/gate at Nailer's Lane.[11]

Monnow Gate's Original Appearance

The Monnow Gate of *circa* 1300 was arguably very different from the present building (Fig. 2). At first glance the gate might be even unrecognizable (Fig. 3), but comparison with today's structure reveals that the changes have been few but prominent. In those days the bridge was considerably narrower, and pedestrians and vehicles passed through the single arched passage of a tower probably whitewashed all over to protect the stonework. The road passage ceiling may have had gothic vaulting springing from the four corners, but no evidence survives of this. The portcullis is shown hanging down between segmental pointed arches. No evidence remains of the type of portcullis winching mechanism that was employed. Often a heavy counterbalance was used to ease dramatically raising of the gate. But, lack of vertical space here would have allowed only a combination of a winch and pulleys (not shown in the drawing) at this gate.[12]

The cross-shaped arrow slits shown are correct for the period. Developed in the thirteenth century from plain loops, the horizontal slits allowed an increased

Fig. 2. Monnow Gate viewed from the
west-south-west in October 1985.

field of surveillance from within. Similar loopholes that are dated can be found at
several sites, including Kenilworth Castle (*c.*1244–66), White Castle (mid-1200s),
·Chepstow Castle (around 1270–2), Caerphilly Castle (around 1277), Usk Castle
(around 1289), St Donat's Castle (around 1300), Leybourne Castle (1300 or a little
before), and Carisbrooke Castle (1335). Although the width of the slits is
deliberately narrow to prevent the entrance of projectiles, it has been demonstrated
in experiments at nearby White Castle that from twenty-five yards an experienced
archer could shoot *into* a plain arrow loop with thirty per cent success. Horizontal
slits would improve visibility for defenders but, also, would improve the success of
attackers. Thus, the cross loops with staggered horizontal slits sometimes found
elsewhere may have been a compromise combining increased visibility with
improved defence. Although hand guns were appearing in the 1380s, the slits at
Monnow Gate were intended for archers or crossbowmen. Slits designed or
modified to take guns had oillets far larger than those present here.[13]

   At first Monnow Gate was without the three machicolation arches that today
form such a prominent part of its façade. The two sets of corbels that support
these arches spring from the wall over the road arch that is directly *behind* the
grooves remaining where once the portcullis hung. They cross through the plane
between the grooves, effectively blocking the pathway of any portcullis gate.
Thus, under this arrangement, coexistence of machicolation and a portcullis is

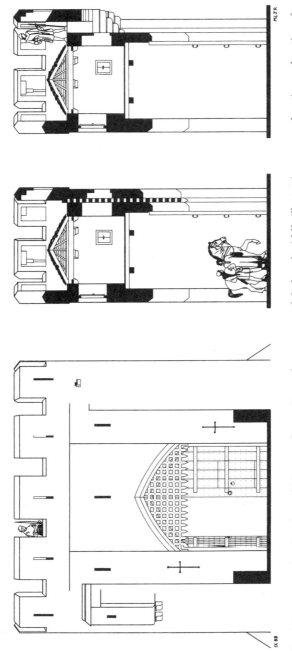

Fig. 3. Reconstruction drawings of Monnow Gate as it may have appeared. Left and middle illustrations are an elevation and section of the gate when first erected. The right section shows the gate after addition of the machicolation.

hardly likely. Only a portcullis mutilated by vertical slots could be used, and this would seriously weaken the gate and its effectiveness. Rather than the machicolation and corbelling now present, commonly a second arch and wall would have crossed directly in front of the portcullis chase making a double wall enclosing a slot for the portcullis. However, here at Monnow Gate there is evidence to suggest that the front of the portcullis may have been exposed, as seems to have been the case at the main entrance of nearby White Castle.

Over the portcullis winching room would have been a roof of low pitch hidden behind a crenellated parapet around a wall-walk (Fig. 4). The roof was supported on stone corbels projecting from the tower room walls. Many types of roof covering are known to have been used at the beginning of the fourteenth century. For low-pitched roofs ingress of water was often a problem, so sheets of lead became a popular though expensive covering. However, tilestones similar to those now existing on the tower were also in use. At Kidwelly Castle the fourteenth-century gatehouse now has a low-pitched roof of tilestones, although in 1422 it was roofed in lead.[14] Around the roof, particularly at the front of the building, there was a narrow wall-walk behind a crenellated parapet. From this elevated position defenders could view and fire upon the enemy with a certain amount of safety. The raised portions of the parapet (the merlons) may have contained arrow loops so that defenders would be less exposed to fire.

Stone machicolated parapets may have arisen independently. But it is tempting to see them as a natural progression from the wooden fighting galleries at the top

Fig. 4. Monnow Bridge and Overmonnow from a view of Monmouth by John Speed early in the seventeenth century (Speed 1610).

of tower walls that were carried outside of the wall top upon wooden joists at early medieval castles. These wooden galleries, at wall-walk level, were used locally at Chepstow and Usk Castles. They may have been removable and only erected in preparation for defence. The next development was stone corbelling at the joist holes to assist in support of the beams. At Caldicot Castle, for example, several of the towers exhibit rings of these hole/corbel combinations. In the final development, towards the end of the thirteenth century, rather than woodwork, stone was being used in the form of arches or lintels to make a permanent projecting parapet with chutes behind each span. Not until the fourteenth century did provision of machicolation become common, and, of course, conversion to stone machicolation tended to lag a little behind that choice for new-built work.[15]

It is difficult to date the addition of machicolation to Monnow Gate since no surviving documents mention the change and the design itself cannot be dated easily to a particular time. In France, similar arched machicolations carried on consoles of two or three stepped corbels existed on fortified churches from as early as the first half of the twelfth century. In Britain though, such a design is now less common. When fortifications were despoiled, particularly following the Civil War, parapets and machicolation were often the first features to vanish. Innumerable defensive towers at castles and gates remain today in a reasonably good condition up to wall-walk level where the parapet features were ruined deliberately in order to render them useless. Being under the parapet, sometimes machicolation arches survived. Machicolation of comparable design to that at Monnow Gate can be found in Britain on a number of towers and gates dating from the late fourteenth century, although this does not imply that all similar machicolations are of that time. Several castle gatehouses in South Wales have triple machicolation arches over the entrance, including Carmarthen Castle (after 1409), Llawhaden Castle (late 1300s), and Kidwelly Castle (shortly after 1400). But, these are broad, flattened, almost horizontal, arches. Machicolation most like Monnow Gate's arches are found at gateways dating over a broad span. At Cooling, Kent, John de Cobham received the King's licence to crenellate and fortify his manor in 1380/1. Subsequently between 1381 and 1386 de Cobham erected Cooling Castle with an outer defensive gate, the twin tower tops of which are encircled with bold round machicolations each on three stepped corbels, strikingly similar to those at Monmouth. Elsewhere in Kent is similar machicolation surrounding a surviving corner tower at Scotney Castle (1378–80), and five deeply stepped arches over the entrance at Hever Castle (1340 or 1384). Likewise, in Sussex, Sir Edward Dalyngrigge erected his Bodiam Castle soon after a licence of 1385. Here again twin towers flank the gateway with more machicolated parapets. Thomas Woodstock's additions of the gatehouse and Woodstock Tower at Caldicot Castle also show finely crafted machicolation dating from 1386. Here, though, the arches are almost pointed rather than round, and, rather than having several conventional voussoirs (arch stones), each arch has only two curiously shaped converging stones. At Leeds Castle, Kent, a date in the 1380s appears yet again, this time for the addition of machicolation to the gatehouse of *c.*1280–1300. On the Isle of Wight, at Carisbrooke, a projecting parapet on five arches was added to the gatehouse of 1335 as late as *c.*1470. These arches also have paired voussoirs.

Monnow Gate's machicolation is rather unusual since, except for those almost flat arches in Wales mentioned above, surviving machicolation elsewhere in Britain often has each arch composed of only two voussoirs distorted by extremely long intrados and extrados faces. That is, a round or slightly pointed arch is formed through two elongated stones rather than through the use of several conventional voussoirs. Also, where portcullis and machicolation coexist, the machicolation consoles were built generally into that wall directly in front of the portcullis chase rather than behind it, and machicolation was much higher since between archway and wall-walk there had to be sufficient space to accommodate the raised gate.

Borough Charters, Tolls, and the Fee Farm Rent

Besides everyday use to enter and leave the town, and occasional use in defence, Monnow Gate and the other town gates were used regularly over more than five hundred years as the sites of toll collections. Tolls were authorized in the patent rolls of 1297 and 1315, and, in subsequent Monmouth charters tolls were allowed for various specific purposes.

In 1256 Henry III had granted a collection of privileges to the burgesses of Monmouth. But, not until 17 July 1447 (25 Henry VI) was Monmouth granted a comprehensive charter of incorporation.[17] In view of the extensive loss, burning of houses, and other oppressions that the Welsh had inflicted upon the town, Monmouth was considered 'waste and desolate for want of burgesses dwelling there'. The 1447 charter allowed Monmouth burgesses a Commonalty from which could be chosen a mayor and other officers who could act as a single body. Amongst the many privileges allowed to Monmouth Corporation was one far-ranging grant of tolls:

We have granted also to the said burgesses, their heirs and successors for ever, our Town and Borough of Monmouth, with its markets and fairs, stallages, picage, dues, censes, and all other customs, profits and commodities belonging to them, as also the dues and toll of the countryside around, and the rent of assize of the burgages, and the castle coules in the aforesaid town and borough and precincts.

The Castle Coules was a tax upon ale brewed for sale in the town. Until this charter the brewer had forfeited a portion of the brew when the King, his heirs, or the Council were in residence at the castle. In their absence a toll was paid.

Toll taking was also greatly assisted in the 1447 charter by prohibition of markets and fairs outside of the borough. In the words of the charter, 'no markets or fairs shall be held within five miles of the borough, in circuit of the same, and ... the market shall be held within the borough walls in the usual and accustomed place every Wednesday and Saturday weekly'.

In return for the multitude of blessings that this charter offered, the Fee Farm Rent was created. This sum of twenty-seven pounds was paid by the Corporation in two instalments annually on the feasts of Easter and St Michael the Archangel. It is extraordinary that the payment continued to be paid to the King and his assignees, more or less regularly, up to 1927, when at last the Corporation made a substantial payment to release itself from the obligation.

Only one hundred years after 1447 many of the privileges were confirmed in the Monmouth charter of 3 Edward VI (30 June 1549). The preface to the charter states that this was necessary since in recent times the town had lost many of these rights, making the borough virtually dissolved and discorporate.[18] Most rights in the 1447 charter were reiterated, and a further fair was allowed just before the clause on the Fee Farm. Thus, on Tuesday, and for two days immediately following in the week of Pentecost, a fair was allowed, the tolls of which were to be applied expressly towards the repair and maintenance of a bridge and certain defences. In the copy manuscript at Monmouth Borough Archives the clause reads,

... concessimus etiam prefatis Burgensibus heredibus et successeoribus quod ipsi habeant annuatim die martis et per duos dies immediate sequentes in ebdomada Penthecost unas nundinas tenedas infra muros Ville predicte Et quod tollagia earundem nundinarum collegantur per Majorem Ville predicte pro tempore existentem et per sanam discretionem Burgens ejusdem Ville disponantur in et circa reparationem et sustentionem Pontis Waye ibidem et januarum Ville predicte Reddente inde annuatim nobis et heredibus nostris per manus Receptoris nostri de Monemouth pro tempore existentis viginti et septem libras ad Festum Paschae et St. Michis. Archi. per equales portiones pro omnibus servitis et consuetudinibus et demandatis.

A transcript, also at MBA, based upon another original copy then at the Chapel of the Rolls, differs slightly from this. Similarly, two manuscript translations at MBA render the wording differently. In the various versions, we have the toll proceeds being applied to some or all of the following: town roads, town bridges, the Wye Bridge, town gates, and the Way Bridge. The original document at Monmouth, quoted above, clearly benefits the town gates and Wye Bridge; although, in 1819, the Town Clerk, Thomas Phillips, interpreted unequivocally Way Bridge (*Pontis Waye*) as Monnow Bridge. But, whichever way the clause was interpreted, tolls collected at Monnow Gate returned there in the form of maintenance and repair at the discretion of the burgesses.[19]

Very soon after Edward's charter the benefits brought to Monnow Gate by tolls were largely lost by the cancelling of these in the charter of 4 James I (14 February 1607). The charter deals entirely with tolls, apparently revoking them in all places for all inhabitants of the Lordship of Monmouth, although foreigners were barred from this privilege.

Wherefore we straightly bid you jointly and severally that when these presents are seen you permit all our tenants, also inhabitants and residents within the towns and lordships of Monmouth, Hardwicke, Skenfrith, Grosmont, and White Castle, and in all portions of the same, which are parcels of the said our Lordship of Monmouth and their servants, to come and go freely, with all and each their goods and chattels and merchandise at whatever fairs, markets, towns, and places, wherever and whenever it shall please them, without any toll, pannage, ferriage, custom, stallage, tallage, tollage, pesage, picage, murage, or land tax being taken from the same tenants or anyone of their servants.

Only thirty-four years later, however, Charles I resurrected the tolls of old in t. Duchy for Duchy residents. The Monmouth charter of 17 Charles I (16 July 1641) commands that all and each of the tenants and residents of the Duchy of Lancaster do pay the tolls, pannage, taxes, etc., as they had hitherto been accustomed to paying. Charles II confirmed the privileges contained in the Edward VI, Philip and Mary (1557), and the James I (1605) charters in letters patent of 1665.[20]

It is peculiar that although tolls within the Duchy for Duchy of Lancaster residents had been abolished and resurrected, by the end of the seventeenth century the situation had become again confused and in dispute. With the Fee Farm Rent obligation ever over its head the Town Council was in favour of charging tolls of all having goods for sale regardless of their place of residence. A precedent was set in 1705 with the case of Price versus Lucas and wife. The plaintiff was Moore Price, a farming tenant of the Duchy of Lancaster from Ty Ucha at Llanvihangel Ysterne Llewerne, in the Hundred of Skenfrith. Price was carrying barley on his gelding for sale at the Monmouth market. He refused to pay toll for the barley before crossing Wye Bridge into Monmouth, claiming that as a resident of the Duchy he was immune from all tolls. Thus, Joan Lucas, wife of the Wye Bridge toll-keeper, a corvizer, distrained the horse and the three bushels. Price brought an action in the Court of Common Pleas against Lucas and his wife, and the Council considered it advisable to defray their costs. Price claimed immunity from toll according to an Act of Parliament of 2 Henry V and in a patent under the Duchy seal of 2 Anne. The defendants claimed that Duchy tenants were immune elsewhere but subject to toll within the Duchy itself, citing a decision in the Duchy Court of 1618. The outcome of the action is unknown. Counsel's opinion by H. Bennett was indecisive though tending to the view of toll immunity except within the Duchy.[21]

Several accounts exist which list the tolls taken on fair days from vendors entering Monmouth with goods. On 8 June 1767 six shillings and seven pence halfpenny was taken at Monnow Bridge, £3.19s.9d. being the income for the day. Likewise, at the Whitsun Fair in 1782, 9s.10d. was levied at the bridge. This figure, plus the money from Thomas Howell, plus eight shillings and seven pence halfpenny taken at the horse fair, minus one shilling each for the toll takers and ale for the workmen, left the handsome profit of £2.10s.11d.[22]

Civil War

Monmouthshire was firmly Royalist during the Civil War, influenced by the House of Worcester at Raglan Castle. The Earl of Worcester had bought the Lordship of Monmouth in 1631, and he remained loyal to the Crown as well as to Rome. Monmouth itself held an important position on the route from Gloucester into South Wales, and, as such, during the war the town was taken and retaken repeatedly by the opposing sides who wanted to control this gateway. A survey of 1610 found the castle to be mostly 'Ruynous and in decaye'.[23] Monmouth's town walls also appear to have been in some disrepair early in the century. However, the town gates were still maintained, and they proved valuable in defence of the castle and borough. With the approaching conflict the town defences were reinforced and some restoration occurred at the castle.

Several Civil War references survive that detail usage of Monnow Gate and the other gates during the unrest. Our first example, concerning Wye Gate, mentions the drawbridge there. At this date Wye Bridge had existed in stone for some considerable time. Any drawbridge at that gate probably crossed part of the town ditch at Wyebridge Street and not the river itself. Thus, on 26 September 1644 Royalist officer Lieutenant-Colonel Kyrle returned from the Forest of Dean with one hundred chosen horsemen, and, arriving at Wye Gate, demanded that Colonel Holtby, the Governor, let down the drawbridge there so that Kyrle could deliver one hundred prisoners. Kyrle, of Walford Court, was a gentleman who changed his allegiance several times during the war. On this occasion once they had gained entrance to the town, Kyrle and his men changed colours and overpowered the guard. The taking of Monmouth in this devious way was an embarassing blow against the Royalists.[24]

Later in 1644, Major Throgmorton had been entrusted with the town of Monmouth for Parliament. Unwisely he sallied forth with three hundred of his most able men to assist in a raid upon Chepstow Castle. In their absence, early on November the nineteenth a motley assemblage of horse and foot from Raglan, Abergavenny, Llangibby, Goodrich, and Hereford approached the town from the north led by Colonel Somerset. Here the town defences were incomplete. Other than the gates, all that protected the borough was a rampart and fosse earthwork. The six sentinels at Dixton Gate took flight, 'whereupon one took an iron bar with which he broke the chain, forced open the gate, and so let in their whole body of horse'. The garrison of two hundred men was retaken, mostly in their beds. Monmouth was once again lost by the Parliamentarians. But, they took consolation in the fact that much of the Monmouth force was still intact due to the foray to Chepstow.[25]

Later, Monnow Bridge receives a brief mention during a Royalist attempt to recover Monmouth early in 1645. Four hundred of the Royalist foot-soldiers arrived from Raglan. This force

gained the bridge having killed the Centry thereupon, by which meanes they possessed themselves of the loopeholes, yet neverthelesse Colonell Kirle drew up his forty men to the Bridge and having beaten the Enemy from it he flanked it on either side in the meane while the Enemies have got over the water, and became masters of our outworkes, and advanced into Monnow streete . . .[26]

After calling reinforcements from the castle, Kyrle eventually drove the Royalist force back over the river and out of the town.

The war ended in Monmouthshire with the seige and surrender of Raglan Castle in 1646. Kyrle, who was still thriving and on the right side when the war was over, occupied Monmouth and proceeded to make its fortifications useless. According to the diary of Monmouth School usher More Pye, on 30 March 1647 'the townsmen and soldiers began to pull down the Round Tower of the Castle, and to demolish the Works'. Then on 22 December Pye records that 'this day, about 12 o'clock, ye Tower of ye Castle of Monmouth fell downe, upon one side, whilst we were at sermon'. No accounts survive of whether or not the town walls and gates were affected during the slighting. It is likely that these were left largely untouched since the object was to make garrisoning of the castle untenable and not to make the town totally defenceless.[27]

Monnow Gate as a Dwelling

Whether or not the war had any effect upon Monnow Gate, by the turn of the century it was in sore need of maintenance and in 1705 Monmouth's Common Council 'ordered as afd That the present chamblains of ye said Town do forth with cause Monnow Gate and the Gates thereof to be repaired and fitted up' (Fig. 5).[28] Until this point there is no evidence that the gate had ever been fitted out or used as a dwelling. It had been a gatehouse only occupied in times of unrest, and, although the original portcullis was long lost, the battlemented parapet and other defensive features were preserved for use as the need arose (Fig. 6).

Once the gate had been repaired, one simple method of ensuring upkeep was to have a gatekeeper resident on site. In this way the porter would be at hand continually and the conditions of tenancy could include provision of repair and maintenance. Thus, dating from November of 1705 we find one of the longest and most fascinating of original documents bearing upon Monnow Gate – an indented contract containing lease of the gate, allocation of the post of porter, and conditions regarding conversion to a house (Fig. 7 and Appendix B).[29] To extract the contract – the agreement was made between the Corporation of Monmouth and Messrs Roger Rosser, a carpenter; and Mathew Bibee and Henry Bibee, sons of the innkeeper James Bibee. The property concerned was 'all that peece of building comonly called Monow Gate Situate on Monnow Bridge', along with

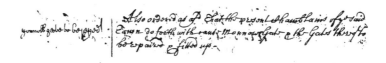

Fig. 5. An order for the refitting of Monnow Gate in the Monmouth Common Council Minutes of 8 October 1705.

Fig. 6. A bird's-eye view of Monnow Bridge and Monmouth from the oil painting *Troy House* by J. Smith, *c*.1700. The viewpoint is taken from a site just above Newton Court, north-east of the town.

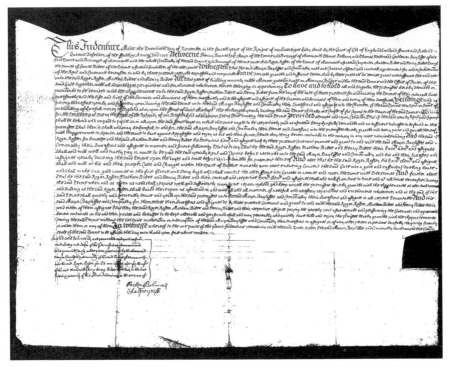

Fig. 7. The contract of 20 November 1705 in which the Borough leased Monnow Gate to Messrs Roger Rosser, Mathew Bibee, and Henry Bibee, along with the position of Porter of the gate.

the office of porter of the said gate. This agreement was to last for the lives of the said Rosser, Bibee, and Bibee, and for the lives of their offspring in perpetuity. In return the lessees were required to pay yearly to the Corporation the rent of one shilling at Michaelmas and a pair of fat capons to the mayor at Christmas. Roger Rosser was further required within the following year to 'Convert the said Gate into a good and sufficient dwelling house' and to 'make two good roomes in the first floore one story high' and to 'convert the other Floore into Garretts or roomes and cover the same with Tile stones'. Finally, the trio was required to sufficiently maintain, repair, and uphold the premises. If the conditions were not met, then the Corporation reserved the right to re-enter and repossess the property.

It is at this time then that Monnow Gate made a great leap towards the appearance that we know today. Rebuilding of the battlements and raising of the roof allowed the gate to be used as a house with all of the conveniences common at the time – no running water, although that was close at hand; the garderobe as an efficient drain and lavatory; and a fireplace. The 1705 contract required the lessees to convert the gate into a house, but, beyond this remodelling of the tower itself, a two-floored extension was constructed which abutted the gate at its eastern corner (Fig. 8). This lean-to extension, timber framed, with lath and plaster infill, projected out over the river, held aloft by a wooden beam and a stone pillar. Illustrations during the century that the extension existed consistently render it as a two-floored dwelling, and no doubt communicating with the gate. One dissenting view is the *Bell Inn* painting by Norfolk artist John Crome (Fig. 9) in which an inn sign hangs from the extension. Crome visited Monmouth on a couple of occasions just after 1800. Beyond Crome's *Bell Inn*, which is also fictional in some other respects, there is no further evidence that the extension was employed as any type of business premises.

Bridge Maintenance and the Chamberlain's Accounts

Although the upkeep of Monnow Gate had been passed on to tenants, the Corporation was still responsible for maintenance of the roadway and bridge. The state of public roads and buildings was reported upon regularly to the Borough Quarter Sessions. When necessary this body then requested the appropriate person or business to take appropriate measures. In that part of the Quarter Sessions' proceedings dealing with presentments in the various town wards Monnow Bridge was frequently named as defective. From 1723 to 1725, and many times subsequently, the bridge was declared 'defective and from ye foot of ye Bridge ye Causeway to dryBridge', and it was 'out of Repaire', along with the 'Way Leading from Monow Bridge to ye Redhill', and 'Alsoe the Gout by Monnow Bridge'. In the case of the town bridges, rates were employed to raise the finance for upkeep. In April 1719, for example, the Quarter Sessions ordered that 'a sum not exceeding the rate of one penny per pound shall be leavied on the Towne & libertys of Monmouth & the hamlett of Wyseham ... for & towards the repaire of Wye bridge & other bridges belonging to the same Towne & libertys'. Rates were also levied for repairs to Monmouth bridges in 1725, 1728, and 1732.[30]

From the earliest surviving Corporation minute books, late in the seventeenth century, we begin to see occasional notices of repair requirements, and orders for repairs to public buildings. Later in the 1700s bills and receipts for works at the bridge are particularly numerous. The fact that these documents are preserved may be as much a result of chance as evidence that more attention was given to the structure in that period.

Like the order for fitting up Monnow Gate, soon after its occupation the Common Council agreed to have the bridge itself repaired.

It was then unanimously agreed upon and order'd by ye sd Mayor Bayliffs and Comon Councill That the Chamblains. of the said Towne do forthwith cause the great Causeway over agst. the mkthouse. and also Monow bridge to be pitch'd and repaired,

Fig. 8. Henry Edridge's (1769–1821) water-colour drawing of Monnow Bridge viewed from Monnow Street in 1808.

Fig. 9. *Bell Inn*, an oil painting of *c*.1805 by John Crome (1768–1821).

And that ye money to be expended by them in that behalfe shall be allow'd them on their accompt.[31]

The yearly accounts of several stewards survive which list all of the income and expenditure of the Corporation. These documents are often detailed with lists of properties let, the tenants, the amount of rent paid or in arrears, the income from tolls at fairs, expenditures on the materials and labour of public works, and the salaries of public servants. For example, Mr Thomas Bellamy's accounts as steward for the year 1709/10 include several entries for Monnow Bridge maintenance.[32] These include:

	£	s	d
pd Lucke Prosser for Irons to fasten monow			
bridg gate	00	01	06
pd Richard green and other laberers for Raiseing			
sinder stuff to lay on monnow bridg	00	13	00
pd Walter Williams wife for 35 Lode off stone			
to pitch ye bridg	01	15	00
pd for haleing the sinder stuff for the			
pitching upon being 17 Lode	00	14	02
pd Will Pigg for pitching the bridg	01	08	06

As above, most references to maintenance are concerned with upkeep of the road surface rather than repairs to the parapets or the bridge underside. Military and slave labour, along with efficient design, had ensured durable roads for the Romans. In more recent times advances in road design by engineers Tresaguet, Telford, and McAdam, and the provision of civil servants responsible for upkeep, again brought about waterproof, impervious road surfaces. The use of tar and asphalt did not appear until the 1830s. Prior to these innovations, roads either required frequent remetalling with broken stones, or they became riddled with pot-holes and quagmires; hence, regarding Monnow Bridge, the common references to the Corporation paying for loads of stone, gravel, and pitching.

In the years immediately after 1705 we find also entries in the accounts for Roger Rosser's one shilling rent. The John Middleton accounts for 1714 indicate payments for masonry work at Monnow Bridge. Also, in that year Rosser's rent was in arrears. It is unlikely that he was evicted. However, the lease was reassigned in 1727. On surrender of the 1705 lease, in another indentured lease of 11 November 1727 Monnow Gate was assigned to Henry Barnes, Baynham Barnes, and John Barnes for the same annual rent of 1s. and a couple of hens for the mayor.[33] Baynham and John were sons of Henry, a mercer, who was mayor of the town in 1705, 1714, 1722, and 1736. As Barnes was a councillor and a man of means, it is likely that one of his sons actually took up the tenancy, or the gate and post of keeper may have been sublet.

Like Roger Rosser in former years, several subsequent chamberlain accounts show payments of 1s.0d. from 'Henry Barnes gent', for example in 'John Middleton's Rents for 1729' Barnes's shilling appears. In 1730, however, it would

appear that Barnes paid rent to himself. In order for the Corporation to relieve a
substantial debt, in September of that year Henry Barnes and the Corporation
entered into a mortgage agreement wherein Barnes was created Receiver of the
Corporation rents, out of which the debt was to be paid. The Borough Council
ordered that 'the Town Seal be affixed to a Deed of Mortgage from the Mayor Bailiffs
& Comonalty. of this Towne to Henry Barnes for the Sume of Two hundred thirty &
seven pounds three shillings & one penny'. It was further agreed and ordered

that the said Henry Barnes be appointed Receiver of the Rents & arrears of Rents & profitts
of the Lands belonging to this Corporation due & payable at Michaelmas next out of which
said Rents arrears of Rents & profitts the said Henry Barnes is to pay to Margaret Baylis
widow the Debt due to her & contracted during the sd. William Rea's mayorality and also
the further Sum of nine pounds due to Mr. Costly for the Repair of the Maces and that what
money shall appear to remain in the hands of the sd. Henry Barnes after paymt. of the Debt
due to the sd. Margaret Baylis & Mr. Costly is ordered to be payd by order of Councill.

Mr Barnes retained control of Monnow Gate. In his will of 30 August 1740
amongst other bequests he leaves to his son, John, the leased house situated on
Monnow Bridge.[34]

Militia Guardroom and Lock-up
During the eighteenth century several documents refer to Monnow Gate and
Bridge as the lock-up, watch-house, bridewell bridge, or the militia guardroom.
Monmouth possessed a town gaol, at first within the castle, later at St Stephen's
Gate in Monnow Street, and then in Agincourt Street. Although a town might
have a proper gaol for the detention of criminals prior to trial, it was also common
to maintain one or more lock-ups for the temporary detention of miscreants. With
only one entrance and no accessible windows at ground level Monnow Gate
fulfilled this role admirably. Although the gate had been converted to a dwelling,
some part of it, or the adjoining lean-to extension, must have been earmarked for
use when required as a lock-up or guardroom. The original role of the militia was
as a reserve for the army and as defence for the homeland. However, in the first
half of the eighteenth century, the militia was employed mainly for law
enforcement. In 1723 fifty shillings were paid to William Blower, 'Keeper of ye
Gaole of this Towne . . . for ye maintenance of ye soldiers lately quartered in this
Towne with fire and candles in ye prison or watchhouse' on Monnow Bridge.
Then in 1732 the Borough Quarter Sessions ordered a rate of two pence per pound
be paid by all inhabitants and landholders for and towards the repair of Chepstow
Bridge and 'the Bridewell Bridge in this Towne', undoubtedly referring to
Monnow Bridge. In 1768 the gate was still employed by militia. Then, James
Powell Naylor took up a lease of the Corporation house adjoïning Monnow Gate
as a dwelling for 10s. a year. However, the conditions required that he vacate the
building whenever it was required as a militia guardroom. As late as 1792 the
militia still paid £3 for rental of the guardhouse (Fig. 10).[35]
    As noted above, it was probably during or following the remodelling of

Fig. 10. Monnow Bridge with militiamen in the late 1700s. A water-colour by Heneage Finch, 4th Earl of Aylesford (1751–1812).

Monnow Gate after 1705 that the extension standing over the river was erected. This extension appears to have been used as a dwelling throughout its short life span. But, the use of the gate itself changed. For some time after its initial refitting it remained a dwelling, with occasional occupation as a lock-up or by the militia. 'Sargant Ross' received a stock, lock, and nails for the 'Tower Store Room on Monow bridg' in 1767. Except for the repetitive evidence that from 1705 up to the early 1800s at least some part of Monnow Gate and the extension were under residential tenure, the surviving documents can seldom show explicitly which parts of the building were set aside for which purpose. Naylor's lease of 1768 clearly refers to the house adjoining Monnow Gate as a dwelling. It is probable that for much of this period the entire structure was a house, with a room, or perhaps the whole building, earmarked for official use when required.[36]

Repairs and Maintenance

Beginning in the 1740s, almost innumerable receipts and vouchers survive from the period up to the time of Queen Victoria. Few of these record deliberate structural changes. Instead they are for provision of glass, a new fire grate, floor-boards, tiles, etc. For the bridge itself there are pointing of the arches, masonry repairs, loads of metalling for the roadway, and rental of boats and pumps to assist pointing works.

Either as part of their pay, or as additional enticement, there are notations of considerable refreshment costs amongst the 'Lodes of Gravile' and feet of ashlar stone. A vague reference appears in Mr Williams's bill of 19 August 1768. There is a charge of 4s.8d. each for William Paul and James Evans's work laying stone and gravel at the bridge, then 1s.6d. 'for drink for them'. An unknown number of men consumed twenty-six quarts of ale whilst repairing the bridge in 1772, then James Baker claimed from the Corporation £4.19s.9d. for 'Liquors to the Workmen while Repairing Monnow Bridge delivered at sundry times'. In 1774 masons Thomas Williams and John Watkins spent six days in 'ye River' presumably repairing the piers. Along with a carpenter, their refreshments accounted for thirty shillings – a considerable sum considering that the masons were otherwise paid only two shillings per day.[37]

The Monnow Gate tenants were required to keep that structure in good order. But bridge and some gate repairs still fell to the Corporation until 1835. It is this situation which caused the preservation of so many receipts and vouchers which, if retained in the hands of individual tenants, would have perished. We see, for instance, that the gate and extension were reglazed in 1763. In all, thirty-five feet of green glass were used. Then 'Charles Plumer' installed leading and '4 Dozen of Quorries'. Other maintenance works include provision of elm boarding, six wain loads of chats, ninety-nine feet of oak floor-boards, whiteliming, window shutters, a new fire grate, pantiles, fencing, and twenty-four pounds of lead.[38]

The period 1771 to 1775 witnessed a comprehensive repair and renovation campaign affecting both the bridge and the gate. As well as the recurring deliveries of road metalling, which were a never-ending requirement, the parapets were repaired with new ashlar stone, decaying stone was replaced under the bridge arches, and the joints of the arches were pointed. Bridge works required construction of a partial dam, a pump, shoring poles, and, from 16 August 1773, the use of a boat at 2s.6d. per week for nine weeks.[39]

Surviving vouchers can be quite informative, with notations of the ordering officer, the contractor, the work undertaken, prices of goods and rates of pay, as well as the exact date on which the works were carried out. During this repair campaign, for example, the then Chamberlain, William Tanner, ordered building stone, and the resulting voucher reads as follows:[40]

> 1773 Mr Wm Tanner –
> to Wm Smith D
> Augs' ye 23th 36 Stones at 1s per peec
> for the use of the Corperation
> to mend monmow Bridge –
> Octobr. 6:1773 Recd of
> Wm Tanner the full   £1"16"0
> Contents pd Wm Smith

The Corporation's main building contractor at that time was Thomas Roberts who, along with his team of masons (James Jones, John Gunday, Evan Hughes, John Richards, Bill Williams, Bill Jones, Mosis Jonson, John Ford, Thomas Williams, and Daniel Watkins), worked at the bridge for six weeks. Each man's rate of pay throughout was two shillings per day. Carpenters appear to have enjoyed the same rate. William Tanner's other role was that of carpenter. He submitted a bill to himself for seven days carpentry at 'monabrige' in September 1773 for the sum of fourteen shillings.[41] Tanner's voucher is ambiguous since the exact nature of the work is not specified. Carpentry could be employed equally to erect timber centring for arch repairs as well as work inside the gate and extension. Receipts suggest that the major works on the gate had occurred earlier, in May 1772.

Renovation of the Monnow Gate in 1772 began with the delivery of 200 flat tiles from Elizabeth Vaughan on 5 May. Then, throughout May, William Price, a 'Tyler', and his men worked on and off with 1,000 tiles (Fig. 11). The glazing 'don at the Gardhous at Monnow Bridge by the orders of Mr Tanner' on 16 May was the installation of fourteen feet of green glass. Elsewhere in the building James Baker, a masonry contractor, engaged in masonry work on 8 and 9 May, installed a beam and made good a wall on 11 May, took down the old chimney on the 12th, built a new one on the 13th to 16th, inserted a door frame on the 18th, laid a hearth stone and walled up a window on the 19th, and on the 20th he repaired a wall. At two shillings and ten pence per day the bill of one pound eleven shillings and twopence was settled in August. For the new fireplace a grate weighing twenty-four pounds arrived on the 15th. Benjamin Maddox later had to make good the floor. His bill, paid in November, is written in a manner at odds with the English of today, though not at all unusual considering the diverse spelling and grammar of the eighteenth century. In part his invoice reads:[42]

May 20th

To 10 fot and a half of forest stone for a hafspas at the gardhows and the stone for to go under the dor frame at 6 ^{d} per fot ———————————	0=5=3
To one man ¾ of a day a making god the flwoer at the gardhows when the chimley was carried up ———————————————	0=1=3

After the 1770s repairs continued, although these were more often improvements or rearrangements of the accommodation rather than works to redress the damages of vehicles or conflict. One exception was the replacement of coping stones in 1783. A mason spent four and three-quarter days laying forty-nine feet of coping whilst another fixed the stones with fifteen cramps.[43] A virtual works hiatus then reigned for twenty years.

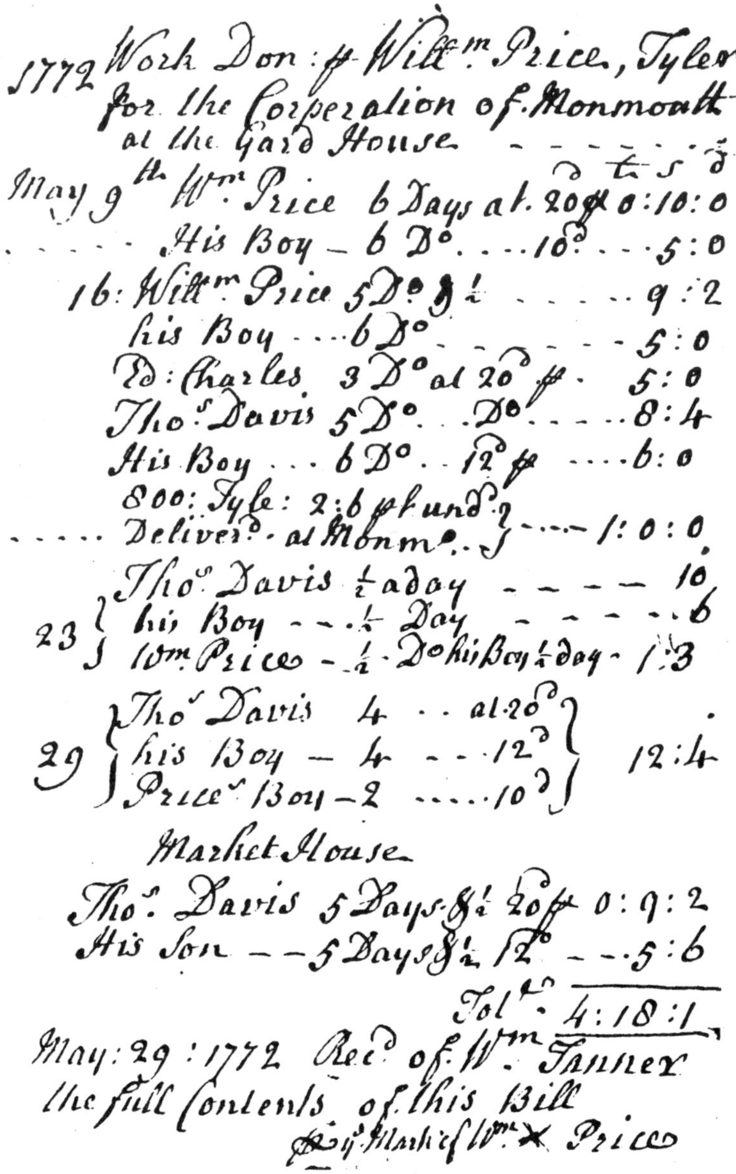

1772 Work Don ḍ Wiᵐ Price, Tyler
for the Corperation of Monmouth
at the Gard House ‒ ‒ ‒ ‒

                                   ᵈ £ s ᵈ

May 9ᵗʰ Wᵐ Price 6 Days at 20ḍ 0:10:0

‒ ‒ ‒ His Boy ‒ 6 Dᵒ ... 10ᵈ ... 5:0

16: Wiᵐ Price 5 Dᵒ ġ ¼ ‒ ‒ ‒ ‒ 9:2

    his Boy ... 6 Dᵒ ‒ ‒ ‒ ‒ 5:0

    Dᵒ: Charles 3 Dᵒ at 20 ḍ · 5:0

    Thoˢ Davis 5 Dᵒ ... Dᵒ ‒ ‒ 8:4

    His Boy ... 6 Dᵒ .. 12 ḍ ‒ ‒ 6:0

    800: Tyle: 2:6 ḍ und ⎫
‒ ‒ ‒ ‒ Deliverᵈ at Monmᵒ ⎭ ‒ ‒ 1:0:0

    ⎧ Thoˢ Davis ½ a day ‒ ‒ ‒ ‒ 10
23 ⎨ his Boy ‒ ‒ ½ Day ‒ ‒ ‒ ‒ 6
   ⎩ Wᵐ Price ‒ ½ Dᵒ his Boy ½ day ‒ 1:3

    ⎧ Thoˢ Davis 4 ‒ at 20ᵈ ⎫
29 ⎨ his Boy ‒ 4 ‒ ‒ 12ᵈ ⎬ 12:4
   ⎩ Priceˢ Boy ‒ 2 ‒ ‒ 10ᵈ ⎭

           Market House

Thoˢ: Davis 5 Days ġ ¼ 20 ḍ 0:9:2

His Son ‒ ‒ 5 Days ġ ¼ 12ᵈ ‒ ‒ 5:6

                  Totˡ 4:18:1

May: 29: 1772 Recᵈ of Wᵐ Tanner
the full Contents of this Bill
              ḍ of Markᵏ Wᵐ ✗ Price

Fig. 11. A receipt for William Price's tiling work 'for the Corperation of Monmouth at the Gard House' dating from May 1772.

Whipping at the Cart's Tail

Whipping was a popular means of punishment in Britain from before the Conquest. The punishment was administered at whipping posts in public squares, in prisons, and at cart's tails. Under Henry VIII vagrancy increased when the refuge of monasteries was abolished. In 1530 the Whipping Act was passed in order to discourage vagrancy. Under the act it was prescribed that the offender should be tied naked to the end of a cart, then, as the cart was drawn slowly about the town, he or she was whipped until the body was bloody. Amongst the public this painful spectacle was quite popular, and crowds would usually develop whilst the punishment was under way.

Alterations were made to the statutes in Elizabeth's reign so that offenders could maintain propriety from the waist down. At this time, also, whipping at the cart's tail began to give way to whipping at a post. The whipping of female vagrants was prohibited in 1791. In the early 1800s whipping began to die out, although as late as 1820 it was necessary to give statutory immunity to all women.

In Monmouth, petty crime likewise resulted often in a whipping, the cart's tail being favoured over a post. Here the Monnow Bridge was a popular departure point for a painful journey as slowly as possible up to Dixton Gate or across to the Wye Bridge. John Howell, a Monmouth labourer, was sentenced for feloniously stealing a silver spoon worth ten pence in 1768. He was to be 'stripped from his waist upwards and publickly whipped from Monnow Bridge to Dixton's Gate at the Cart's Tail & till his Back is bloody'. By 1788 sentences had become harsher. On 14 July William Edmonds was found guilty and was sentenced to a similar fate as Howell. However, his crime was one tenth as heinous. He had been charged with 'feloniously stealing taking and carring away one piece of Cheese of the value of one penny of the Goods and Chattels of Charles Tyler Gentleman'. It is curious that the said gentleman also served on the Grand Jury.[44]

A crime involving a ten pennyworth cloth cloak was considered in January of 1790. The entire proceedings were recorded as follows:

Monmouth   The General Quarter Sessions of the Peace of our Sovereign Lord King
Town   held at the Guildhall in and for the said Town and the Libertys
thereof on Monday the Eighteenth day of January in the thirtieth year of the Reign of our
Sovereign Lord George the third King of Great Britain &^{c}. and in the year of our Lord 1790
Before Thomas Hughes Esquire Mayor and William Powell and Herbert Phillips Esquires
Bailiffs of the said Town and those of his Majestys Justices of the peace Assigned to hear
and determine divers Felonies Trespasses and other Misdeeds Committed and done
within the said Town and Libertys thereof one of the Quorum

Names of the Grand Jury

Luke Phillips		William Roberts		Philip Powell
James Yarworth		John Hughes		John Painton
Charles Tyler	Sworn	William [illegible]	Sworn	James Dowding
William Jones		Benjamin Yeats		William Davis
Samuel Morgan		George Duberly		William Kinson
		Isaac Billings		

. . .

At the same Court William Godwin was Indicted for Feloniously stealing taking and carring away one Cloth Cloke of the Value of Ten pence of the Goods and Chattels of Ann Harris

John Beazley		Thomas How		John Badham	
Thomas Burrow		Charles Ford		Richard Taylor	
William Farner	Sworn	William Good	Sworn	Hugh James	Sworn
William Rosser		Philip Thomas		John Anthony	

Guilty

Ordered that the Overseers of the Poor of the parish of Monmouth do pay to Ann Harris the sum of One pound and one shilling for the prosecuting William Godwin for Felony

Ordered to be publickly Whipped at the Carts Tail on Saturday next from Monnow Bridge to Wyebridge and on that day Month to be publickly whipped at the Carts tail from Wye Bridge to Monnow Bridge and to continue in Goal three months ...[45]

One suspects that after two whippings and a three month detention Mr Godwin refrained from stealing any more cloth cloaks.

Although of a much later date, and not resulting in a whipping, an interesting case referring to Monnow Bridge occurred before magistrates in 1854. On 22 April of that year Esther Jones was brought before the bench to answer charges of soliciting on the bridge. William Fuller, a police constable, made a sworn statement as follows, 'I saw the defendant last night on Monnow Bridge, she was soliciting persons for the purpose of prostitution'. Forthwith Jones was punished by a fine of 40s. and costs of 2s.6d., or imprisonment for one month. She went to gaol.[46]

Wye Valley Tours and Topographical Prints
Dissolution of the monasteries and the Civil War were two great creators of British ruins. For a century after the acts of 1536 and 1539, the iconoclast period saw religious houses spoiled and stripped of their treasures, and not least of these treasures was the plentiful supply of lead on church roofs. Stripping and melting down of this material soon led to ingress of the elements and the onset of decay. Fortifications suffered a similar fate. The beginning of the war saw the militarization of defensible castles and houses along with the rapid restoration of neglected structures. However, once captured by Parliamentarian forces, many of these buildings were slighted and made indefensible. This slighting, though, did not raze the castles. As at Raglan and Goodrich, the castles remained substantially intact but largely incapable of defense or even accommodation. Monmouth Castle's slighting was much more drastic, though it was soon followed by the erection of Great Castle House out of the ruins.

By a century later these churches, abbeys, and castles had become romantic decaying focal points for the cult of the heroic British past, encouraged by the likes of Wordsworth, Dyer, and Gilpin. A growing appreciation of the mystical qualities of nature, the attraction of these crumbling ruins, and eighteenth-century antiquarian zeal brought hordes to Monmouthshire to partake of the Wye Tour. In Gilpin's account of his excursion in 1770, dusk at Monmouth becomes a surreal scene.

During many miles we kept upon the heights; and, through a long, and gentle descent, approached Monmouth. Before we reached it we were benighted: but as far as we could judge of a country through the grey obscurity of a summer-evening, this seemed to abound with many beautiful, woody vallies, among the hills, which we descended. A light of this kind, though not so favourable to landscape, is very favourable to the imagination. This active power embodies half-formed images; and gives existence to the most illusive scenes. These it rapidly combines; and often composes landscapes, perhaps more beautiful, than any, that exist in nature. They are formed indeed from nature – from the most beautiful of her scenes; and having been treasured up in the memory, are called into these imaginary creations by some distant resemblances, which strike the eye in the multiplicity of evanid surfaces, that float before it.[47]

Wye Valley tours generally started at Ross, travelling down to Chepstow by boat, with stops to view sights, and an overnight stay at Monmouth. As today, the picturesque attractions included Goodrich Castle, Symond's Yat, the Seven Sisters Rocks, Monmouth, iron and tin industries at Redbrook (now defunct), Tintern Abbey, and the Wyndcliff. Frequent stops were made to examine these features, along with tasteful repasts above vistas and amongst ancient crumbling monuments.

Several lyrical accounts of the tour were published in the later 1700s. William Gilpin's *Observations on the River Wye, and several parts of South Wales* goes about analysing the outing by his own special rules of picturesque beauty. His lofty purpose was not merely of describing the various sights,

but of adapting the description of natural scenery to the principles of artificial landscape; and of opening the sources of those pleasures, which are derived from the comparison. Observations of this kind, through the vehicle of description, have the better chance of being founded in truth; as they are not the offspring of theory; but are taken warm from the scenes of nature, as they arise.

A more down-to-earth account came from Monmouth printer Charles Heath in his *Excursion Down the Wye*. Poets had their say also, reflected most famously in William Wordsworth's 'Lines, composed a few miles above Tintern Abbey, on revisiting the Banks of the Wye during a Tour, July 13th, 1798.'[48]

> These beauteous forms,
> Through a long absence, have not been to me
> As is a landscape to a blind man's eye:
> But oft, in lonely rooms, and mid the din
> Of towns and cities, I have owed to them,
> In hours of weariness, sensations sweet,
> Felt in the blood, and felt along the heart;
> And passing even into my purer mind,
> With tranquil restoration ...
> O sylvan Wye! thou wanderer thro' the woods,
> How often has my spirit turned to thee!

In this same period when Wye tours were enjoying popularity, reflected by tour accounts and the muses, generally a widespread interest was growing in the study and appreciation of ancestral piles and historic buildings as a pastime. Several series of descriptive topographical works were published, from Heath's historical and descriptive account of Monmouth to the encyclopaedic set of volumes of Britton and Brayley's *The Beauties of England and Wales*.

In those days, when travel was much more laboured, photography had not yet developed, and the means for touring holidays were restricted to a small fraction of the population, illustrated books were for many the only taste they would ever have of such as the sylvan Wye, the romantic ivied ruins of Raglan Castle, or relics at Monmouth. In works from the 1770s to the 1830s a large number of topographical drawings and prints of Monnow Bridge were produced. Except for the detailed and annotated drawings of the bridge of few like the architectural historian John Carter (Fig. 17), the surviving late eighteenth-century pictures of the structure are sketches that are often romanticized and too vague interpretations. They commonly suffer from artistic licence and the fact that, unlike the artist, the engraver of a topographical book had possibly never seen the subjects of the pictures. Often the engraver's burin had to create precise lines and stipples from the artist's washed over details and murky shadows.

An example of the distortions sometimes concealed in engravings can be seen in Figures 12 to 14. Figure 12 is of an unattributed copper engraving. It is entitled *The Monnow Bridge*. But, except for the existence of a gateway on a bridge, the

Fig. 12. An anonymous engraving depicting Monnow Bridge.

Fig. 13. An engraving of the bridge by S. Noble after a sketch by P.S. Munn.

Fig. 14. A pencil sketch of the bridge by Paul Sandby Munn (1773–1845).

resemblance to the real structure is weak. Above the gate there are no machicolation arches, and the building attached to Monnow Gate appears very ambiguously. The reason for this undistinguished rendition is that in this instance the engraver probably copied another engraving, not an original drawing. The first generation engraving was executed by S. Noble (Fig. 13). Noble's print is dark and romantic. It is easy to see how ambiguous parts of his interpretation became even more vague in the later print. The Noble print was published in the Monmouthshire volume of *The Beauties of England and Wales* in 1803, and it reproduces a drawing by Paul Sandby Munn (Fig. 14). When compared to other evidence it is clear that Munn's drawing is accurate, bearing in mind that this is a quick pencil sketch which omits some detail. These missing trifling details were later re-created by the engravers so that a complete picture could be presented.

John Ireland painted a water-colour sketch of Monnow Bridge in 1794, one year before J.M.W. Turner drew a pencil sketch during a Wye Valley tour. The results differ considerably in content as well as style. The aquatint of Ireland's drawing (Fig. 15) suffers from similar problems to the Noble/Munn engraving. Ambiguities in Ireland's washy sketch (now preserved at the British Museum) caused the engraved main arch to appear published almost as a segmental pointed arch, the three machicolation arches to be rendered pointed, and a spurious window to appear under the eaves. Turner's view dispenses with washes, rendering the view entirely in pencil (Fig. 16). The result is a precise picture, unspoilt by secondary interpretation, and reflecting a bridge and gate in many ways indistinguishable from the structure standing today.

Drawings and engravings of the bridge were made by Samuel Prout, A.V.C. and T.H. Fielding, David Cox, Francis Grose, the Varleys, J.S. Cotman[49], and J.M.W. Turner, along with numerous lesser-known artists such as George Samuel, H. O'Neill, T.C. Hofland, and Edward Blore. For historians, contemporary views can be invaluable in re-creating the past appearance of this or any other monument. However, bearing in mind the distortions illustrated above, no non-photographic illustration can be relied upon without corroborating evidence from independent illustrations or independent documentation.

Loss of the Lean-to Annexe
By the beginning of the nineteenth century Monnow Gate remained essentially the same in structure as it had been in 1706. Heath's description of 1804 indicates that the accommodation above was reached via a circular stair of twenty stone steps. There was by then a single room thirty-six feet long and ten feet wide. The gate itself had been abandoned as a dwelling, and its only purpose was as an occasional guardhouse or powder room for the militia whilst stationed at Monmouth.

Accurate and sometimes detailed illustrations exist of the bridge and gate at

Fig. 15. *Monmow Bridge*. An aquatint of Monnow Bridge viewed from the south, published in 1797.

this time by John Carter (Fig. 17), Samuel Prout (Fig. 18), John Varley, and Henry Edridge (Fig. 8). Looking at these reminds us that the bridge still remained at its original width, the pedestrian passageways had not been created, and the lean-to annexe survived. Also, the river bank on the south side of Monnow Street had not yet been built up during creation of the cattle market.[50] This low natural bank remained up until the later 1870s, contributing to the apparent height and grandeur of the ancient river crossing.

The first major structural change of the century came when the century-old lean-to building was demolished in 1815. Some time had been spent in August 1814 in mending holes in the 'Pears' (piers), cramping and pointing the piers, and repairing the bridge spandrels. The reference to cramping may account for the seven large cramps securing ashlar work on the tower pier near water level. Between June and August 1815 the 'auld house' at Monnow Gate was pulled down and the bridge made good. Messrs Watkins and Benson stripped the house at the beginning of June, taking any reusable materials off to the warehouse. The resulting hole in the bridge parapet was then filled, coped, and cramped. Four feet of stone were required in July whilst fitting window bars at the gate. Then an

Fig. 16. A pencil sketch of the bridge viewed from the west, made by J.M.W. Turner (1775–1851) in 1795.

effort was made to make good the gate by inserting new ceiling joists over the road archway on 17 August, along with lathing, 'wight washing and plaistering'.[51]

A.V.C. Fielding made a sketching tour along the Wye in 1816. His drawing of the bridge sans lean-to was later engraved by his brother T.H. Fielding and published in their part-work *A Description of the River Wye* in 1818.

Historically the Monmouth Corporation had been responsible for upkeep of the bridge itself. This situation was confirmed in the Paving Act of 1818. A body of commissioners was formed to execute the conditions of cleansing, lighting, maintaining, and watching the Monmouth streets as detailed in the act. The whole was to be funded by a general rate. With regard to bridges, their repair, maintenance, and support was to remain the duty of the body responsible before the act was passed (on 3 June 1818). Monnow Bridge might well have fared better if it had come under the commissioners' remit. The act decreed that streets under their control that required repair were to be repaired immediately following the defect being brought to their notice. They were to notify their

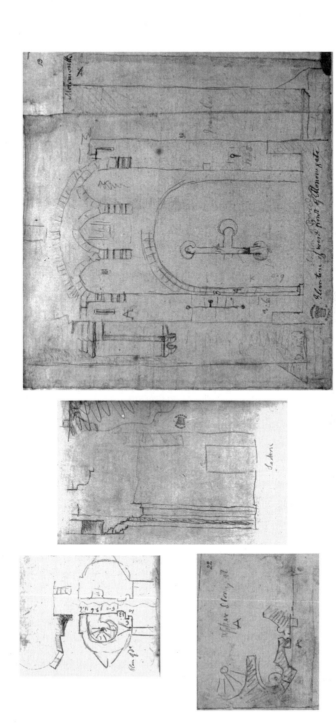

Fig. 17. Plan and elevation drawings of Monnow Gate made in 1801 by John Carter (1748–1817).

Fig. 18. An engraved view of Monnow Gate published as plate 59 for the book *Rudiments of Landscape* by Samuel Prout (1783–1852).

paving contractor, who, if he neglected to effect repairs within five days, was liable to forfeit to the complainant a sum not exceeding twenty shillings per day. If the act was executed with zeal, then Monmouth's streets must surely have been constantly clean and in impeccable order. However, although the commissioners were able to collect an average of £240 per annum, by 1833 the commissioners had accumulated a debt of £1648.8s.11d., and arrears to the amount £154 were due from more than one hundred rate defaulters. The town was 'tolerably paved and cleansed', but the public services that suffered in consequence were the town lighting and the provision of watchmen.[52]

Pedestrian Passageways and Widening of the Bridge
It is now difficult to comprehend that the roadway at Monnow Bridge could have been so congested in 1819 that a separate pedestrian passage was necessary. But, such must have been considered essential, otherwise major works would have been avoided. Considering that the lean-to building had been removed in 1815 (Fig. 19), it would have been logical to pierce the downstream side of the tower with a passage. This would have avoided

Fig. 19. *An Old Gateway at Monmouth*. An unusual view of Monnow Bridge from the north, after Thomas Hofland (1777–1843). The engraving is based upon a sketch made between 1815 and 1819.

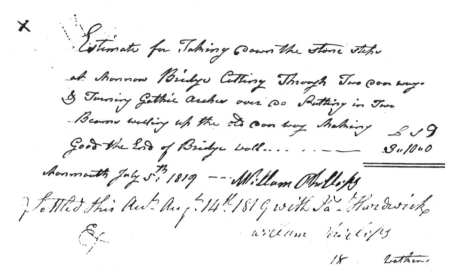

Fig. 20. An estimate for building the gothic style pedestrian passage at the bridge, dated 5 July 1819.

destroying the stone newel stairway in the upstream side. However, in July 1819, an estimate was submitted to the Corporation for creating a passageway where the old stair still stood (Fig. 20), quoting £3.10s. for taking down the old stair, cutting doorways through each side of the tower, erecting gothic arches, putting in two beams, walling up the old tower entrance, and making good the bridge parapet. The project went ahead during that summer between July and the end of October.[53]

Piercing the tower for a passage began with brute force to break off the newel stairs and to break through the walls on each side. 'Raking Gothick centers' were made to support the two arches at 5s.3d., then the side walls were made good to create a slightly serpentine passageway. A flagstoned ceiling was applied, leaving the rest of the stairway in ruins above. This completed the suitably medieval style passage, except for the walling above the gothic arch facing Overmonnow. Here the stonework was not properly repaired, remaining rough until a restoration programme in the 1890s.

Being several years before the bridge was widened on that upstream side, the new passageway was actually through part of the tower outside the bridge sides. A small platform was needed at each end so that pedestrians could reach the passage. On each side of the tower the parapet was breached and platforms were built with metal railings and stone paving. The platforms seem to have rested upon timber beams bridging the gap. This is suggested by the surviving

Fig. 21. *Bridge over the Monnow, Monmouth*, a water-colour drawing by T.E. Rosenberg (1790–1835), dating from the early 1820s. Both this water-colour and the engraving after Gastineau depict the cross-shaped arrow loop incorrectly; Gastineau or Deeble drawing a complete cross, and Rosenberg completely omitting the loop.

papers and by comparing the contemporary drawings and engravings (for example, a water-colour view by T.E. Rosenberg (Fig. 21), and the engraving after Gastineau (front cover illustration). Webb and Webb (1879) also reproduce an illustration dated 1823).

Once the original gate entrance and stairway had been destroyed, then it was necessary to build a similar structure at the other side of the roadway. Carter's 1801 drawing appears to indicate a doorway as the entrance to a store-room on this side. Nevertheless, a new doorway was made with another new gothic style arch over, and an oak jamb. An elm door was hung, and within the tower a two-flight oak stair was constructed, costing £1.7s.9d. The project was completed in October when some oak flooring was replaced, oak shutters were placed over the windows (3s.6d.), and ten iron bars secured those windows in the loft (1s.9d.).[54]

Little work occurred in the 1820s beyond the usual pitching of the road, plastering, and the repair of some tiling. The one dramatic change was the widening of the bridge on the upstream side *c*.1827.[55] George Delamotte's pencil sketch view from Monnow Street shows the bridge before the widening of any parapet on the Monmouth side (Fig. 22). The gothic passageway is there but the old parapets remain at the original positions. To the right are the cottages between the Barley Mow public house and the

Fig. 22. Pencil sketch of Monnow Bridge by George Delamotte dated October 1826.

Fig. 23. David Cox's (1783–1859) etching of Monnow Bridge viewed along the roadway from the south-west, dated 1827.

bridge which stood until demolition in the 1950s. In 1827 David Cox appeared on the scene, and his sketches resulted in a superb, detailed soft ground etching (Fig. 23). By this time the first widening had occurred, carried on new arches springing from the cutwaters and abutments. These three new arches carried a footpath the full length of the bridge on the upstream side, making unnecessary the old pedestrian refuges over pier two. Since so far the downstream side was untouched, here the refuge remained intact. All of Cox's etching is supported by other evidence, except for an anomaly in his garderobe. Here his rendering of the passage to the garderobe suggests that there was a boarded wooden door out of the passage to the exterior. Also, Cox appears to indicate an arrow slit/peep-hole at the lavatory itself. A tiny window at a garderobe was a frequent feature in medieval times. It provided ventilation and allowed the defenders to be ever vigilant, even whilst answering the call of nature. But, except in David Cox's view, no other account, pictorial or written, supports a door or slit at the garderobe of Monnow Gate in the early 1800s.

Since sole access to the tower room was now via the stairway at the

Fig. 24. *The Old Monnow Bridge, Monmouth*, a steel engraving by J. Newman.

downstream side of the tower, piercing of this side for a pedestrian passage arch was avoided. In November 1830 the bridge was widened along the entire downstream side. Instead of constructing another pedestrian passage through the tower, a platform was constructed so that pedestrians could pass *around* the tower (Figs. 24 and 26). The upstream parapet had been built mostly with new stone and with new chamfered coping. But, downstream the wall was rebuilt using much old material. As with the previous widening, arches were thrown across between the cutwaters and the abutments allowing a parapet and footpath above. The parapet wall slightly overhangs the bridge sides, and this overhang was 'supported' by twelve plain rounded corbels.[56]

In 1832 the downstream footway was completed and the gate's dilapidated roof was rebuilt (Fig. 25). The roof was taken apart, rebuilt as before except for the creation of deeper eaves, and it remains essentially unchanged. It is during this rebuilding that the dormer window to the rear was lost and eight massive corbels were introduced. These stone supports are in fact made of brick rendered over to resemble true stone. The proper purpose of corbels is to support a weight. But these support nothing and one can only imagine that they were created to improve the tower's appearance in some way (Fig. 26).

In this decade responsibility for the maintenance of Monnow Bridge passed

Fig. 25. *New Roof 1832*. A drawing of the writing in chalk made by a workman on the northern principal rafter of the south-eastern roof truss at Monnow Gate.

from Monmouth Corporation to the County. Thus, in the General Rules for the Court of Quarter Sessions, the duties of the Surveyor of County Bridges are outlined, along with a list of these structures. Although the Court of Quarter Sessions had taken an interest in Monnow Bridge for some time, the transfer of charge in September 1845 led from the Municipal Corporations Act. The surveyor was required to report upon the condition of every county bridge at each Quarter Sessions. Any repairs or improvements recommended by the surveyor were then approved by the Court; two magistrates handled payments, and the surveyor examined the contracted work. As with the numerous routine receipts and vouchers in the eighteenth century, routine and repetitive surveyor's reports and subsequent Quarter Sessions orders in the mid-nineteenth century list the bridge as being in tolerable repair, requiring roadstone, or requiring pointing.[57]

Messrs Cave and Rolls were instructed by the Court of Quarter Sessions to examine the downstream parapet and footpath of the bridge in 1844. Then, in March 1845, instructions were given to prepare a new footpath and archway 'so as to pass through the Tower at an expense not exceeding Five Pounds'.[58] The new pedestrian passage could not have gothic arches to match the upstream side since the height of such arches would complicate the design of a new staircase to be incorporated with the passage. Insertion of the passage jambs and lintels required setting back of the adjacent wall projection. The quoins of the projection above are supported by an inserted corbel on the north-east side and by stepped stones on the south-west. In order to accommodate both a passage and access to the tower room, the lower part of that access had to be extremely compact. Thus, at footpath level a brick wall was built to divide off the chamber, with a narrow flight of steps inserted between the pedestrian passage and the road passage. Once above the pedestrian way the extra space allowed a wooden circular stair to be used. Creation of this second pedestrian passageway was the last significant

Fig. 26. An engraved view of Monnow Bridge from Monnow Street before the downstream pedestrian passageway had been built and after rebuilding of the roof.

structural alteration effected to the bridge or gate. Since 1845 the structure has remained essentially unchanged, the subsequent works being primarily ones of maintenance and repair (Fig. 27).

Monnow Gate under the Duke of Beaufort

The brass plaque attached to the front of Monnow Gate, along with the feudal role of the Somersets, has led people to the erroneous conclusion that the Dukes of Beaufort had some ancient claim on this monument. However, the Monnow Gate was directly associated with that family only from 1830 until 1900.

In the former year, the Corporation desired to build a new watch-house for Monmouth, and a small property at the bottom of the Beaufort Arms yard appeared ideal. After negotiations with the Duchy, on 12 October the Town Council ordered

that Deeds of Exchange between his Grace the Duke of Beaufort and the Corporation be prepared at the expence of the Corporation for vesting in the Corporation the Tenement and land now belonging to His Grace upon which the new watchhouse is intended to be built, and for vesting in His Grace the present Lock up house on Monnow Bridge which His Grace has consented to accept in exchange.

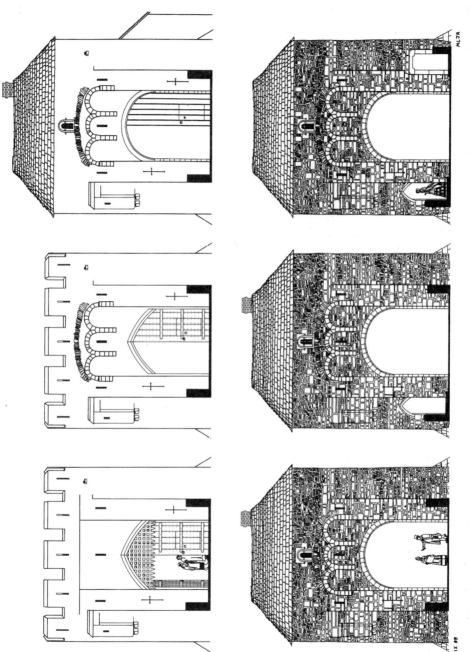

Fig. 27. The development of Monnow Gate in a pictorial summary. Along the top row – the gate as it may have appeared soon after 1300, in about 1400, and after the conversion to a dwelling begun in 1705. Below – the gate after demolition of the lean-to in 1815, before 1830, and after 1845.

Due to an oversight the exchange was neglected. This led eventually to the town clerk reminding His Grace in a letter of 15 December 1835.[59]

For the remainder of the century the gate continued in disuse, or at most in use as a store-room. The gate of 1837 is described as being in a dilapidated state by the *Western Mail*'s Special Correspondent in an article on old Monmouth. However, the article is a fifty-year retrospective of the town in Victoria's jubilee year. The correspondent also describes the Church of St Thomas as dilapidated. This is questionable since only six years beforehand Arthur Wyatt, the Duke of Beaufort's agent, had orchestrated a complete refurbishment of the church.[60]

The gate's exterior was exploited on occasions as a place from which to fly flags and streamers, and hang hoardings. During June of 1838 the coronation of Queen Victoria was celebrated in Monmouth and the thoroughfares were decorated with triumphal arches of oak, laurel, and flowers, surmounted by crowns and stars. Considering that Monnow Gate's defensive role was intended against attack from without, it is peculiar that during these festivities apparently it was used to prevent exit. Following a service at St Mary's Church, the 'Mayor of Overmonnow' proceeded in a coach drawn by four horses to his 'borough', as a splendid cavalcade

moved through Church-street, Agincourt Square, and Monnow Bridge. Here the object of His Worship the Mayor of Over-Monnow in leaving the Church before the procession began, was made known. His Worship, in assertion of an ancient claim, had closed the portcullis of the gate, and the Temple Bar scene was enacted, of the Herald of the Mayor of Monmouth, with flourish of trumpet, demanding admittance for the Mayor. The Herald of the Mayor of Over-monnow, with like "flourish", ordered the portcullis to be raised. The procession then moved through Over-monnow, and returned up Monnow-street.[61]

As has been seen earlier, with the machicolation consoles in place it would be quite impossible to incorporate a true and complete working portcullis on Monnow Gate. The coronation portcullis must have been some type of contrivance put up in an effort to reinforce the pomp and ceremony of the grand festival. In modern times a suggestion that a portcullis be re-created came from the Town Council. The idea was quashed, not because it was realized that a real portcullis cannot now be constructed at the gate, but because a new portcullis gate would act as a further traffic obstruction to a building that already obstructs large vehicles quite sufficiently.

An instance of the gate being used as a flagpole occurred during the parliamentary elections of 1847. Lord Granville Somerset had been the victor and the celebrations in Monmouth were tumultuous, far beyond the tepid observations of today. As Somerset toured the town a band led playing 'See! the Conquering Hero comes' along a route under arches proclaiming 'Lord Granville for ever', 'Civil and Religious Liberty', and 'God save him'. Much of Overmonnow had supported Somerset's opponent. Thus, noticeably, there the houses were not festooned in garlands of oak boughs, laurels, and evergreens. The gate had been flying a banner during the contest, but spoil-sports had removed the flag before the procession. In the following week (28 August 1847) 'Fair Play' wrote to the *Monmouthshire Beacon* newspaper proclaiming that indeed the residents of Overmonnow had not been at all sulky over the outcome. The inhabitants were both cheerful and happy. He continued, writing that the flag hoisted on the tower would have remained had the contest been a 'fair and honourable one'. Instead, members of the triumphal party had in fact paid to have the banner removed early.[62]

At the coming of age in 1891 of John Maclean Rolls, eldest son of John Allan Rolls (the first Baron Llangattock) and brother of Charles Stewart Rolls, similar grand festivities took place. John Allan Rolls, variously a Member of Parliament, Freemason, and Mayor, was Monmouth's greatest benefactor. Sadly, the Rolls sons were later to die prematurely and without issue. Based at the Hendre, over a fifty-year period the family made a profound mark upon Monmouth, most notably leaving to Monmouth the Gymnasium (later referred to as the Nelson Rooms), the Rolls Hall, the Hospital, and a collection of Admiral Lord Nelson relics (now at Monmouth Museum). The Rolls' were generally well liked and the coming of age of the future second Baron Llangattock became another circumstance for celebrations and decoration. Individuals and shopkeepers festooned their premises with shields, flags, and garlands, and banners proclaimed 'Long life, health and prosperity', and 'Long live the heir of the Hendre'. Many gas-lit illuminations were erected along the streets. Mr W.M. Teague had the contract to decorate Monnow Bridge with flags and to illuminate the whole at night with fairy lights.

Another Rolls festival occurred in 1900 when the Duke and Duchess of York came to Monmouth to visit the Llangattocks. Again, decorations were everywhere along the streets. 'Venetian masts, with connecting streamers, lined the roadway in front of the cattle market and on either side of the Bridge. A few trophies were affixed to Monnow Gateway, the Bridge being considered to look better in its primitive condition.' Or, as occupants decorated only outside their own premises, perhaps no one was keen on financing any grand show on the bridge.[63]

Beyond the celebratory flags and lights, Monnow Gate also displayed placards and advertisements. As an uninhabited and little-used building with a prominent position and an absentee owner, it was easy to nail up boards that might be left unhindered for considerable periods. In September 1881 the situation prompted 'Antiquitatis Amator' to write a complaint to the editor of the *Beacon* for the attention of the authorities.[64] However, defacement by advertising placards continued into this century. Even within the pedestrian passages the walls were employed. A glass slide of the 1890s shows clearly an advertisement for Reckitt's Blue nailed on to the wooden beams of the downstream passage. Another in the road passage announces a forthcoming bazaar.

At the turn of the century both Monmouth Town Council and Monmouthshire County Council expressed interests in possessing Monnow Gate. Councillor Lawrence approached the County Council asking to whom the gate belonged. The Clerk to the County Council 'courteously never sent any reply whatever'. The

Town Clerk wrote to the Duke of Beaufort's agent suggesting a transfer of custody to the Town on the basis that the proper authority to own the structure was surely the Council of the town in which it was situated. However, negotiations proceeded between the Duke of Beaufort and the County Council. H.S. Cowper Coles, the agent, informed the Town Clerk that His Grace considered that as the bridge belonged to the County, they would be the proper party to assume custody of the gateway built upon it. Thus, Cowper Coles wrote to the County that His Grace would give Monnow Gate to the County. In August 1900 a brass plaque (Fig. 28) was attached to the front of Monnow Gate to commemorate the presentation.[65]

A Major Repair Programme in the 1890s

After the bridge widenings and insertion of the pedestrian passageways, Monnow Gate and Bridge were neglected for thirty years or so. Little evidence exists of any changes or maintenance work until a major programme across the 1890s. The earliest surviving photographs of Monnow Bridge (e.g. Figs. 29 and 30) show at least the gate to have been a pathetic structure with a catalogue of ills. Stonework above the gothic pedestrian arch had never been made good after 1819, gaping cracks ran down the walls, arch stones had been allowed to slip, and patches of falling-off rendering revealed where heavily eroded masonry had been covered up

Fig. 28. Drawing of the brass plaque attached to Monnow Gate in 1900.

Fig. 29. Photograph of Monnow Bridge viewed from the west, before 1876.

Fig. 30. Photograph of Monnow Gate viewed from the south-west, *c.*1860–70.

rather than replaced. Non-resident ownership of the gate and its lack of use allowed the building to creep close to a dangerous condition. Attention to tilestones falling off in 1883 was a prelude to the most comprehensive conservation/restoration programme in centuries.[66] The programme was not orchestrated as a full conservation project. Nevertheless, by 1902 the bridge and gate had been restored to a better condition than had existed for a considerable time before.

The County Council was responsible for bridge maintenance, and it initiated paving works after the Town Council had complained. An agreement was made in 1889 that if the Town would arrange for kerbing, then the County would lay new stone paving and guttering.[67]

In 1889 or 1890 measures were taken to arrest eventual collapse of the building by its literally falling apart. Since the gate's outer wall is in the form of a flattened ellipse, there is an inherent potential instability if the back and front walls are not tied together by other means. The side walls of the main road arch should fulfill this role. But, under the south-west road arch, where originally there were door jambs projecting from the side walls, the columns of blocks were not properly bonded to the adjacent wall facework. That is, vertical uninterrupted joints run up the walls next to the site of the jambs rather than the stones interlocking. Drastic measures were taken ending in the insertion of metal bars and rods to tie opposing walls together and discourage further separation. Hidden within the tower room's wooden floor are bars which tie the road arch side walls together. Then, more obviously, two tie rods were inserted to tie the front and back walls at the top of the road side walls. The rods can be found within the tower, and the four round plates are conspicuous on the exterior (Fig. 31).[68]

Although a metal bar was inserted partly embedded in Monnow Gate's front wall to tie the road arch side walls together, it is unfortunate that the authorities of the time did not seize the opportunity to go a small step further. The bar was concealed within the floor of the room and partly embedded within the front wall just below the lowest machicolation corbels. Its size suggests that it was intended to serve only as a tie bar and not to bear weight. However, in that same position it would have been hardly more trouble to conceal a substantial girder which could have improved stability vastly. On the front wall much of the weight below the relieving arch is carried by the main road arch. Although in fact the wall above might remain intact with the main arch removed, damage to the arch causes a considerable threat to the integrity of the structure. Naturally, in days of yore when the walling first achieved its current design, threats to the road arch were virtually absent. But, in the century beginning in the 1890s, large motorized vehicles became an ever-increasing threat. A girder would have relieved the road arch of its burden so that any damage to that arch would not threaten the entire work above. This might have obviated the substantial rebuilding works of recent times.

The spring and summer of 1892 witnessed long-awaited attention to the bridge itself. The bridge was closed to heavy traffic in March (Fig. 32) prior to works beneath the spans. In April it was reported in the *Beacon* that the piers, abutments, and arch rings were receiving attention. This work was carried out on the middle

Fig. 31. Close-up photograph of Monnow Gate viewed from the south-west, *c*.1890.

and Overmonnow spans. Centrings were set up to support the spans whilst several arch ring voussoirs were replaced and much of pier two was refaced (Fig. 33).[69] The new stonework is identifiable still by its neatly tooled and fresh appearance.

When the works were nearing completion, the County Surveyor, William Tanner, reported to the County Council on the progress. The original plans to repair stonework were revised when coffer dams were erected at the central span prior to insertion of the centrings. Diversion of the water revealed the extent of river bed erosion as well as undermining of the bridge piers. The bridge closure order was extended immediately to all traffic, and there followed a bed stabilization project one century before authorities repeated the process with different technology. The bed was dug out down to solid material before topping back up to the nominal bed level with coarse poured concrete and sacks filled with concrete. By August the Surveyor's team was well into work at the Overmonnow span, here refacing the pier above and below water level. This left a solid though irregular bed under both spans. Under the Monmouth span the bed was hardly touched since historically this span had been virtually dry due to frequent siltation (see, for example, Figs. 15, 19, and 29).[70]

Closure of the bridge for so many months in 1892 led to inevitable disruption and complaints. The annual May or 'Mop' Fair at Little Chippenham was

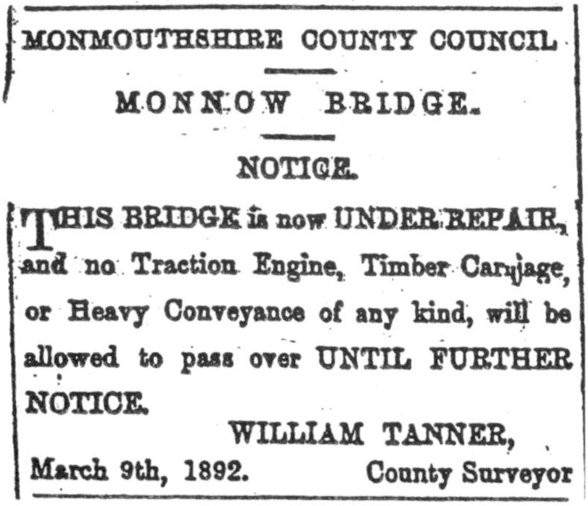

MONMOUTHSHIRE COUNTY COUNCIL

MONNOW BRIDGE.

NOTICE.

THIS BRIDGE is now UNDER REPAIR, and no Traction Engine, Timber Carriage, or Heavy Conveyance of any kind, will be allowed to pass over UNTIL FURTHER NOTICE.

WILLIAM TANNER,

March 9th, 1892.   County Surveyor

Fig. 32. A bridge closure notice from the *Monmouthshire Beacon.*

Fig. 33. Centring used under Monnow Bridge during the span repairs of 1892. A photograph by R. Tudor Williams.

affected since vehicles were unable to cross the Monnow. Thus, in this year the fair was divided between Chippenham and St Thomas's Square.

Studt's switchback, the leading feature in the pleasure fair was located just outside the "Green Dragon", and among the other numerous attractions was Mander's Waxwork Exhibition (à la Madame Tussaud's) which included a portrait of the demon Deeming and other well-known characters, good, bad, and indifferent.

Mr C.H. Portnell, of 10 Monk Street, later wrote to the Town Council complaining that the bridge closure had caused a very heavy deficit in Fair receipts. His demand for recompense was denied since bridge closure was a County concern. Hence, Portnell took his complaint to the County. His letter asking 'for compensation for alleged loss of business through the stoppage of traffic over Monnow bridge, during its repair, was ordered to lie on the table'.[71]

The bed excavations revealed several historical artefacts long concealed in gravel and silt. The pocket pistol by William Henshaw of the Strand (Fig. 34) is a fine late eighteenth-century brass piece with a wooden stock. Another relic found under the bridge may have come to light during these excavations. This is an ancient three-headed stone from a capital depicting a woman, a king, and a devil. The stone's size and orientation suggest that it might have been part of a capital once situated under a church's chancel arch or a south doorway tympanum. Capitals with a similar characterization exist in the Parish Church of St Philip and St James at Tarrington. These date from the second half of the twelfth century. It is conjectured that this stone may once have been part of the fabric of St Thomas's Church. In 1186 both churches are listed as belonging to the Priory of Monmouth, and thus they may

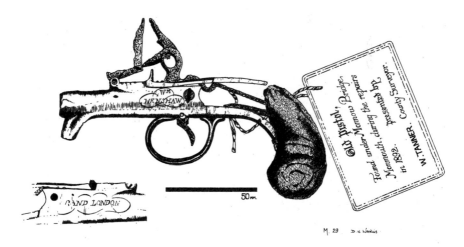

Fig. 34. Drawing by D.N. Watkins of the flintlock pocket pistol made by William Henshaw.

have shared designs or masons. Other likely sources for the stone must be few indeed since only churches and other monumental buildings would be candidates.[72]

A further questionable find of the time was an alleged Saxon coin horde from under the bridge. In Fred Tyler-Taylor's Monmouth history lecture notes of 1903 he states that 'a considerable quantity of coins dating from the Saxon period onwards, & some ornaments said to have been of gold & silver, were found embedded in the clay at the bottom of the river, but they disappeared & have not been traced'.[73] Still their whereabouts are unknown.

Monnow Bridge was reopened to traffic in October 1892. In view of the speed and quality with which the substantial works had been effected, the County Roads and Bridges Sub-Committee recommended that for services rendered the sum of £15 be paid to William Davies, the Clerk of Works. Their gratitude was reflected one year later when condolences were dispatched to his widow. Alderman Parfitt reported that when 'the Monnow Bridge was under repair, Mr. Davies was there night and day to see that the work was carried out to the satisfaction of the Surveyor and to the county'. He had been 'a most faithful and energetic servant'.[74]

Mr P.E. Wanklyn, Surveyor to the Town Council, proposed that Monnow Bridge should be lit after receiving complaints on the dark archway. It is surprising that a lamp hanging in the road arch from the ceiling did not receive support. However, the council did apply to the County for permission to erect a street lamp on the upstream parapet, and on 13 April 1893 the Town Clerk was granted such permission. Thus, over the pier two cutwater, the thickened parapet was employed to support a lamp of generous proportions. Although changing colour from time to time, the lamp (Fig. 35) survived up until the late 1920s when its top portion was replaced by twin electric lamps (Fig. 53). During the 1960s the lamp was shorn off entirely.[75]

More recently lighting was reinstated as the Chamber of Commerce played a role in the installation of permanent floodlighting for the monument, the lights being positioned on the adjacent riverside walls. The bridge was one of six sites selected by South Wales Electricity for the award of a floodlight grant. This was supplemented by a Welsh Tourist Board grant. After some adjustments to diminish the dazzling of drivers, the lighting was inaugurated on 29 July 1991.[76]

Although the gate belonged still to the Duke, the Mayor of Monmouth announced at a Town Council meeting, on 14 August 1893, that Mr Wyatt was leaving the area and he had presented the 'original' (and only) key to the tower to the council. A cabinet of curiosities existed in the Rolls Hall, and it was agreed that the key should be on display there along with other ancient relics.

Necessary maintenance of the gate exterior took place in the middle of the 1890s, finishing before 1897. Despite ownership by the Duke, it is clear that the Town Council was responsible for some, if not all, of the works. Roof guttering and downpipes were added, but most of the full-scale conservation affected masonry over virtually the entire structure. Badly eroded stone was removed and replaced throughout with squared blocks of old red sandstone. Most of these new blocks have a slight 'rock face'. This stone can be seen in particular

Fig. 35. Photograph of Monnow Bridge and Gate viewed from the south-west. Taken by J.H. Thomas at 12.30 p.m. on 13 July 1907.

between the gothic archway and the garderobe. Once recognized, sandstone of this repair programme can be found dotted all over the gate surface. As well as this inserted stone, gallons of mortar must have been required to fill the gaping joints particularly around the walls at the gate sides where accessibility is poor. The attic window was rudely repaired, turning into a shapeless mass of mortar what had until then been a finely detailed design.

One very noticeable change during the repair programme was restoration of the cruciform arrow slit by the cutting of a slot and oillet, making a symmetrical cross. Viewing the front of the gate, the left-hand arm of the cross had been absent from surviving pictures of the gate from the earliest times. The restorers removed the large stone forming the upper left side of the cross *and* the existing right-hand arm. A slit and oillet were cut into the large stone, then it was placed back in position. Strangely, the original right-hand stone appears to have been replaced entirely. Comparison of photographs taken shortly before the restoration (e.g. Fig. 31) with those taken soon afterwards indicate a right-hand stone with a fresh appearance and without the noticeable pits and markings visible beforehand.[77]

Monnow Gate Open to the Public

'A Lover of the Old Town' wrote to the *Beacon* in November 1899 suggesting that the interior of Monnow Gate ought to be made good and visitors be allowed into the ancient pile. This was duly considered during the discussions of ownership that followed shortly. Councillor Lawrence pointed out to the Town Council that many would like to view the tower room but that it had been kept locked up for many years and had served only as a lumber room and pigeon house. He wished to see the gate fitted out as a miniature museum, perhaps with a new window to improve the lighting. In turn Mr Tanner, the County Surveyor, was prepared to leave the key in the custody of Mr Rendell, the Rolls Hall Keeper, so that it could be exhibited. But, the room was inappropriate as an exhibition area and any new window could not be considered as this would injure its architectural features.[78]

The tower room was at last opened for free public inspection in 1902. As final improvements, the unglazed lights had been filled with leaded panes, a flight of steps was placed in the room to enable viewing of the machicolation platform, and a new staircase was fixed. Appropriate furniture was added in the form of an old oak table from Mr J. Hall, builder, and a contemporary upholstered oak chair from Mr H.T. Simmonds. Monmouth artist and historian Mrs M.E. Bagnall-Oakeley began writing a brief history of the tower, and a visitors' book was provided.[79]

The first official visitors to Monnow Gate were headed on 1 May 1902 by Edwin Grove, the Chairman of Monmouthshire County Council, and Hamilton T. Baillie, the Mayor of Monmouth. Later entries in the visitors' book include the Borough Surveyor (10 June), the Postmaster (29 July), and the Town Clerk (21 August). Soon after the official opening, the County's Monnow Bridge Tower Sub-Committee met at the Shire Hall to consider the rules of opening. The minutes report that the

Committee decided on the following regulations for the admittance of the Public which are to be painted on a board outside:– (1) The building to be opened free from 10 o'clock until sunset. (2) Application to view must be made to the Caretaker. A board to be placed inside:– 'The Monmouthshire County Council request that no gratuities be given, and trust that visitors will insert their names in the book provided.' The question of appointing a Caretaker was considered.

An order was given to appoint a caretaker at a salary of £5 per annum. The *Beacon* reported that Miss Violet Lewis of the Robin Hood Inn had been appointed at £25 a year. Later, this report was corrected. A painted sign was prepared indicating the whereabouts of the key (Fig. 36). For many years this hung over the door of 128 Monnow Street, the shop of H. Andrews, confectioner, adjacent to the Robin Hood Inn. The building has since been demolished.[80]

By February 1903 Mrs Bagnall-Oakeley had completed her Monnow Bridge history booklet. The Monnow Bridge Sub-Committee thanked her for her efforts and ordered that the work be printed and distributed. Mary Bagnall-Oakeley appears also to have made further contributions in the form of two water-colours and a patent roll transcript then hung below the wall-walk. The patent roll is a transcription of the translation published in

XI 86   MLJR

Fig. 36. Drawing of the painted wooden notice of the Monnow Gate key location.

Bagnall-Oakeley's 'The Fortifications of Monmouth' and in her tower book.[81]

The tower room had indeed become a miniature museum. Contained in the ancient structure there were furniture, water-colours, the patent roll copy, a small cabinet of antiquities, and loose relics casually placed about (Fig. 37). Other than replacement of the visitors' book in 1927, the only addition to these exhibits was made in 1926. Sir Henry Mather-Jackson, Bt. CBE, presented two

Fig. 37. The interior of Monnow Gate, *c.*1910.

framed photographs for display in the room. These depict Monnow Bridge and a similar contemporary, the *Pont Vieux* at Orthez, France. Some of these relics have vanished during the intervening decades. The whereabouts of the case and its curiosities is unknown.

The gate has remained freely accessible for inspection to a greater or lesser degree. In latter years the key has been duplicated, with the 'original' donated to Monmouth Museum for exhibition only.[82] Usable copies are kept at a remote location, although one remains available for the use of visitors.

Scheduling and Listing

Monnow Bridge and Gate are Listed as a building of special architectural or historic interest and Scheduled as an Ancient Monument. These distinctions afford a statutory protection which, except for the actions of natural decay, should ensure the preservation of this unique structure indefinitely. Inclusion on the schedule indicates a building of national importance. The building was added to the schedule on 12 April 1923 upon the recommendation of the Chairman of the Ancient Monuments Board for Wales. It was registered with the Local Land Charges on 9 February 1934. Then, the building was listed during the resurvey of Monmouth on 15 August 1974. The listing is at Grade I, along with Monmouth Castle, Great Castle House, and Shire Hall, and it denotes a building of exceptional interest. The Grade I distinction is enjoyed by less than one twentieth of listed buildings.[83]

The first ancient monuments legislation came in 1882 with the Ancient Monuments Protection Act, which listed just a handful of structures that warranted statutory protection. The acts of 1913 to 1953 set up most of the rules and infrastructure observed today, with Inspectors of Monuments, Commissioners of Works, and detailed regulations concerning repairs and preservation. The first acts concerned themselves only with uninhabited buildings, often in a ruinous or semi-ruinous state. Not until after the Second World War were measures taken to list and protect complete (usually inhabited) buildings. Listed buildings are subject to control under the Town and Country Planning Acts, recently revised in the Planning Act of 1990. Anyone wishing to demolish, or to alter or extend a listed building in such a way that its character is affected must obtain 'listed building consent' from the local planning authority or the Secretary of State. The procedure is similar to that for pursuing ordinary planning permission. However, in cases where a listed building is also a scheduled ancient monument, the provisions of the Ancient Monument Acts supersede those of the Town and Country Planning Acts. Monnow Bridge is such a listed and scheduled structure.[84]

Legislation affecting scheduled ancient monuments is contained in the Ancient Monuments and Archaeological Areas Act 1979. Any works which involve the demolition, destruction of or damage to a scheduled monument or any part of it, or works for the removal or repair of a scheduled monument or any part of it, require scheduled monument consent before they are authorized. This consent is sought from the Secretary of State, or, in Wales, from Cadw: Welsh Historic

Monuments, now an executive agency which was set up in 1984 and charged with recording, protecting, and conserving historic buildings and ancient monuments throughout the principality for the Secretary of State for Wales. It is an offence to conduct works on a scheduled monument without scheduled monument consent, and any damage to an ancient monument, according to the statute, is an offence punishable by fine or imprisonment. There is, however, a formidable exception to this control. Works may proceed prior to formal consent if they are needed on urgent health and safety grounds; for example, if the structure or part of it can be considered unsafe. This procedure has been exercised at Monnow Bridge.[85]

Planned repair and maintenance works at Monnow Bridge have been undertaken following application for consent. Assuming that the works are approved in principle, the plans and preparations can be assisted by the guidance of inspectors and architects from Cadw. Unfortunately, however, on some occasions the conservation guidelines do not render finished works appreciated by the man in the street. Major works at Monnow Gate in 1989 carried out by contractors for Gwent County Council proceeded under Cadw guidance. But, the finished work, approved by Cadw, suffered considerable public criticism.[86]

Cadw also takes sole responsibility for the care and presentation of some monuments. Where appropriate, public access is allowed following any required consolidation or conservation. At larger monuments Cadw maintains custodial staff on site and interpretative displays are provided.

Collisions and Obstructions
Ever since the beginning of the era of vehicles with internal combustion, Monnow Gate has presented an obstacle to the free flow of traffic. This has led usually just to some minor traffic congestion. But, on several occasions vehicles have either become stuck under the gate or collisions have damaged the tower or bridge. Horses and wooden carriages could do little damage to sound stonework. The almost irresistible power and strength of some modern vehicles have wrought considerable destruction.

The first reported incident of collision was in 1901. On 25 March a procession of Mr John Studt's amusements passed through the town. One vehicle was too high to negotiate the archway. The solution was quite simple – the road was dug up until the carriage was able to squeeze under. Messrs Studt had similar problems in 1926. This time their carriage got jammed in the archway, 'and for a time defied all attempts to get it away'.[87]

The problems at Monnow Bridge for vehicles are multiple. The bridge is hump-backed so that, particularly when leaving the town, drivers cannot see vehicles approaching from the other direction until the last moment. The slope each side combined with a long vehicle led to damage in 1934. A large crane had passed through the gate very slowly so as not to touch the side walls. Yet the rear end of the crane swung upwards tearing along the stonework and gouging holes in the archway ceiling. Vehicles can only negotiate the archway single file, and then the drivers of lorries and large vans must take great care to avoid the side walls and to manoeuvre under the arches at their centre. Scoring of the arch stone soffits and streaks of paint show the number of times that lorries and buses literally have scraped through the gate. Sometimes this has led to movement of masonry and the potential for considerable further damage. As the only road-bridge over the Monnow at Monmouth, Monnow Bridge carried the A40 road and all traffic until recent times. During the Second World War regular crossings by military vehicles led to inevitable accidents. As the bridge carried a crucial road link, necessary repairs had to be rapid and, sometimes, temporary, so that the thoroughfare could remain unobstructed. 'A large lorry, proceeding in the direction of Newport,' on 29 June 1941, 'damaged the archway, several large stones being dislodged. A squad of men had to be called out to effect temporary repairs to keep the bridge open for traffic.'[88]

Numerous accidents occurred also due to the narrow bridge approaches along the bridge itself and down to St Thomas's Square. From the square to the bridge the road is now considerably wider than it was up until the 1920s, with houses standing along the south side and the bridge road width then carrying on down to the square (Fig. 38). To remedy the situation, the Town Council came to the momentuous conclusion that all of the buildings between Monnow Bridge and St Thomas's Church should be purchased and demolished. This would eliminate a blind corner at the square, allow road widening, and perhaps make provision for a second river crossing. Thus, by July 1925 the council had acquired all of the houses along that row. By October the *Beacon* was able to report that the 'houses on the other side of Monnow Bridge are rapidly being demolished, and already the dangerous corner leading to Cinderhill Street has lost its terror for motorists.'[89] In due course the roadway was widened and a garden was laid out on the site of the terrace. In pursuing this programme the roadway became safer and a good vantage point was gained for admiring the monument. Yet, up until 1925 Monnow Bridge had been part of a townscape (Figs. 35 and 4), mobbed by rows of houses since the early Middle Ages. Suddenly it was isolated with a terraced backdrop to the north and west and unnatural desolation to the south.

Two solutions to traffic congestion and safety were considered in the 1930s – a mirror and traffic signals. Ernest Potter recommended that a large mirror be fixed to the archway ceiling. This did not find favour, not surprisingly. In order to see vehicles beyond the brow of the bridge, one probably would need to be so close to the gate that the mirror would be unnecessary. Sensible plans were made for traffic control signals at the bridge, sparked by another letter to the *Beacon*, this one being from 'Safety First'. Of the bridge, Mr 'First' wrote that it 'may be an ancient and picturesque monument worthy of preservation, but in this motor-age when the world and his wife take to the roads, it constitutes a real danger to life and limb both to pedestrians and motorists'. Automatic traffic control signals were the solution, and the Town Council immediately took up the idea. Monmouthshire County Council was approached and consideration was given by the Main Roads and Bridges Committee. The situation at Monnow Bridge was

Fig. 38. St Thomas's Square and Monnow Bridge in the autumn of 1888. The restored ancient cross was unveiled on 20 September 1888 and replaced with a second restoration on 24 December 1888.

examined, leading to the conclusion that signals would improve safety and curtail congestion. Hence, the committee gave approval for the work. Strangely, however, the lights did not materialize, and the issue vanished without trace.[90]

Carrying of the A40 trunk road by the bridge led to inevitable problems for massive lorries during the Second World War. In March 1941 a collision forced repairs to both archways of the gate. Scaffolding was erected so that cars and small vehicles could pass under. Heavy traffic was directed via the Wye Valley or towards Skenfrith. For these large vehicles the bridge was a bottleneck through which one tried to squeeze or face a detour of several miles. Other than consideration of building a replacement bridge, the County Council did put forward a novel and drastic measure for relieving traffic pressure – removal of part of the tower. Bridge width was less of a problem than headroom at the gate. The two main arches and their low sides presented a prominent obstacle; an obstacle which could be removed. The Roads and Bridges Committee and the County Surveyor, Mr S. Bennett, suggested to the Ministry of Transport that the lower portion of the tower be removed temporarily to facilitate the passing of large vehicles. 'This would be a temporary measure and the demolition would have to be replaced after the war because Monnow Gateway is scheduled as an ancient monument and as such, must be retained.' Besides constituting deliberate vandalism to an ancient monument, the proposed works would have been highly complex in order to create headroom and yet maintain integrity in the remaining structure. The Ministry of Transport vetoed the project.[91]

Further damage occurred at the beginning of July 1941. Again, the bridge was not closed completely. However, before the repairs were complete, a lorry leaving town did further damage, knocking newly-set masonry out of alignment. On the evening of the 8th yet another vehicle was unsuccessful in squeezing through. The *Beacon* reports that Joseph Jones, a County Council night watchman, was charged with ensuring that vehicles did not disrupt scaffolding holding up loose masonry. Morgan Fuller James, driving a lorry to London carrying 'important goods', ignored a red light, two notices, and Jones's warning. Although guided by three people, including the night watchman, the lorry succeeded in knocking over the main arch shoring. Later, a case against James of driving without due care and attention was dismissed.[92]

A rare complete closure of the bridge came in January of 1944 when considerable damage was wrought by a lorry to the north-east face of the gate. The heavy vehicle became wedged under the archway, resulting in the removal of arch stones on the left-hand side and damage spreading up to the window overlooking Monnow Street. Damaged walling was roughly reassembled using areas of cement and sand mortar. The window surround received considerable damage. Temporary repairs were effected which were not improved upon later. The surround was rendered over unskillfully with coloured mortar rather than careful repair and conservation. It was left in this state. The other repairs were improved partly during a repair scheme of 1989.[93]

The most far-reaching damage to Monnow Bridge or Gate by a vehicle came on 18 May 1982 when a National Welsh double-decker bus smashed into the south-west front. Single-decker buses were a common sight, carefully manoeuvring through the arch, and possibly accounting for some of the red paint and gouges under the arch stones. But, driving a double-decker bus through is an impossibility. Returning to Monmouth bus depot, the bus, driven by a thirty-four year old Monmouth man, collided with Monnow Gate, wrecking the vehicle and causing unprecedented damage to the building. The upper portion of the bus reached up to the bottom of the machicolation arches, knocking corbels out of alignment and resulting in considerable cracking to the wall over the main road arch and the archway ceiling. Whilst the driver escaped serious injury, the bridge was closed to traffic immediately since clearly the damage had made the gate front unsafe.[94]

Complaints on the inconvenience of bridge closure and that closure would devastate trade and business in Monmouth were taken into account and the County Council introduced overtime working to speed the 1982 repair works. The Ancient Monuments Division of the Welsh Office advised upon technical aspects and the choice of building materials. Yet, there was inevitable conflict between the desire for rapid reopening of the bridge and the need for skilled, careful conservation work.[95]

Although the collision in May caused no major collapse, it was determined that the extent of damage required partial demolition and reassembly. Thus, for the first time in centuries, over the roadway the walling was completely dismantled up as far as the relieving arch. This was done despite the fact that the road arch itself had sustained no appreciable damage, indicated by the fact that no support was given to the arch whilst demolition of the structure above proceeded. Much of this wall above was unscathed also.

When dismantling and rebuilding is necessary it is customary to retain sound masonry, to rebuild to match the original as closely as possible, and, where practicable, to replace stones in their original positions. In all three of these respects the repair works fell short of the ideal, resulting later in a handful of published condemnations.[96]

Once controlled demolition had occurred (Fig. 39), the new roadway arch was constructed springing on each side from the original springing stones. Formerly during this century, when the arch was repaired, individual voussoirs were removed and replaced. Thus, the old arch was a mixture of old and new stones, most of great age, with about one-third of the stones representing twentieth-century replacements (Fig. 40). Rather than salvaging the old voussoirs and reassembling them, all except the springers were discarded in 1982, and a set of twenty-four small, new, Forest of Dean sandstone voussoirs were cut and erected. Although of reasonably correct shape, with a chamfer and rebate, the new stones were diminuitive versions of the ancient voussoirs. The horizontal depth of the new stones fell well short of that of the most intact surviving old arch stones. The intrados and extrados of the stones were also flat, producing an arch intrados of twenty-four flat planes rather than a continuous smooth curve. Furthermore, the stones were hardly wedge-shaped at all, forcing the masons to employ conspicuously V-shaped joints to achieve the arch's curvature. Finally, the choice of stone was inappropriate. Like the ashlar masonry of the gate, the old arch had been composed mainly of red and grey old red sandstone. The new stones were all of a very pale Forest of Dean sandstone which, though they may have been somewhat more robust than old red, continued to be a grating eyesore until their removal in 1989 (Figs. 41 and 69).

Over the new arch the gate's design was reconstructed, although it was argued at the time that the work fell short of conservation standards. Much of the old masonry was reused, but no stones appear to have been placed in original positions. Amongst the changes brought with the new structure were the introduction of recessed joints between stones, stonework built more to courses than previously, and the stones becoming almost 'rock-faced'.

At the machicolation, the three nineteenth-century holes allegedly made at the time of the Chartist troubles (shaped square, rectangle, and rectangle) were rebuilt as two only (square, absent, and square). The eight corbels supporting the machicolation were numbered in chalk prior to dismantling. These were replaced as before, except two had to be replaced by new stones. The machicolation arches themselves were rebuilt in reused stones, except for a new central springer and three new arch stones. Most of these arch stones were replaced in a reversed position, with the former exterior face now facing inward.

Fig. 39. Partial demolition prior to repairs to the tower in June 1982.

Fig. 40. Monnow Gate in July 1975.

Fig. 41. Monnow Gate, 27 December 1985.

Above the roadway the ceiling was transformed. Since the 1820s the two oak beams which support the floor above had been covered by a ceiling which was 'supported' by stone or plasterwork. At each corner on the wall below the ceiling a heavy moulding rose off a console and then crossed the ceiling diagonally to form a strange vaulting which pretended to hold up the ceiling and floor above (Figs. 30 and 40). This was all discarded, exposing the beams and the floor joists. Boarding was inserted between the two timbers, leaving the lower part of each beam visible.

As outlined above, a number of small changes were made to Monnow Gate during the rebuilding of 1982. Individually most of these changes were not of profound significance, and a number are reversible. However, taken together the changes altered the character of the building. The discrepancies could be rationalized by the fact that these were unplanned emergency repairs. In this instance the need to reopen the roadway had a strong influence over the proceedings.

After representations from the Town Council, the Chamber of Commerce, and Monmouth District Council, the County Engineer was able to report in due course that as work on the bridge had been pushed on as quickly as possible, the estimate of ten or twelve weeks to complete the work could be revised. The bridge was reopened on 19 June 1982, just one month after its closure. In order to prevent further catastrophic accidents, the Town Council approached the education authority (whose buses crossed the bridge), the County Council, and the Police in pursuit of a total ban at the bridge for buses and lorries. This was unsuccessful. As before, the restrictions remained at a weight limit of three tons unladen, and an advisory height limit of 10 ft. 3 in., *except* for buses.[97]

The next major occurrence at Monnow Bridge left the gate unscathed. On 28 September 1985 at 11.35 p.m. a vehicle chase through Monmouth resulted in a coal van smashing through the bridge parapet wall. The van was first seen by police-officers driving the wrong way up Whitecross Street, then continuing along Church Street, in which all traffic was prohibited. Subsequently the van careered under Monnow Gate, swerved to the left, and crashed through the parapet wall above pier two, stopping before falling into the river. The driver was unhurt and he left the scene. Later, the driver, from Tredegar, pleaded guilty to a total of ten offences and was sentenced by Monmouth magistrates to six months imprisonment and a fine.[98]

This collision resulted immediately in some twenty feet of the parapet falling into the Monnow (Fig. 42). A further ten feet of loose masonry fell into the river over the next few days, mostly as a result of being pushed. At this time the Monnow was consistently at a high level due to recent heavy rains. Since the old stone was relatively inaccessible, the choice was to proceed with a temporary parapet repair or to leave the hole just fenced until the stone could be retrieved. A wooden fence was put in place until much of the stone was

Fig. 42. The broken downstream parapet after a collision, 29 September 1985. The damage exposes the through-stone foundation of the parapet and its double-skinned construction.

retrieved, and County Council masons were able to proceed with rebuilding of the wall.[99]

The parapet was rebuilt using much of the original masonry, and by late November the repairs seemed to be complete. Again, however, a shower of complaints fell from the Town Council and the public over apparently unskilled work. The parapet had been destroyed down to the string course. In this region two corbels had rested under the course; one fell out due to the accident, and the other had sheared off previously. Neither corbel was reinstated. The parapet was rebuilt without the benefit of scaffolding. Thus, the outer side of the wall, where access was difficult, had some uneven facework and pointing missing from joints between the stones. Discussed in their monthly meeting, the Town Council agreed to write to the County to express their reservations over the parapet repairs, as well as the gate repairs of 1982, and the fact that the council should employ 'qualified stone masons on any future repairs to the bridge'.[100]

Despite strong defence from the stonemasons and the County Council, the Town Council reiterated its complaints over the parapet repair, joined by the Monmouth Action Group, and later by the Welsh Office itself. In a written reply, later published, to the Member of Parliament for Monmouth, Sir John Stradling Thomas, the Parliamentary Under-Secretary of State for Wales, Mr Wyn Roberts, revealed the unusual position of the monument and Cadw's role in protecting it:

'It is evident that the [County] Council view the Bridge as essentially and primarily a means of carrying traffic across the river and are not altogether sympathetic with the need to conserve it through careful repair and restoration work' wrote Mr Roberts. Cadw's Conservation Architect had agreed that some of the recent work carried out to the Bridge was of a poor standard. 'This can be attributed to the fact that certain works in recent years have been required urgently on health and safety grounds, such as following an accident on the bridge, thus obviating the need for formal consent to be granted by the Secretary of State' said Mr Roberts. 'This means Cadw has been unable to exercise the normal statutory procedures and apply its high standards in those circumstances.'

As a result of a meeting between Cadw and council officers, remedial measures were taken on the parapet and some imperfections were corrected.[101]

A New Monnow Bridge
The desire for a new bridge to relieve and replace Monnow Bridge arose due to traffic congestion and an effort to protect the old bridge and gate from damage. The effects of congestion were relaxed in the mid-1800s when pedestrian passageways and paths were created allowing a separation of pedestrian and horse traffic. Along with increasing motorized traffic and increasing accidents on the bridge, calls for a second river crossing began a century later in the 1920s. When in 1925 the terrace of houses south of the bridge was demolished the *Monmouthshire Beacon* welcomed the prospect of a safer road.

The change already effected in this direction is extremely welcome, and we assume that, shortly, the additional bridge across the Monnow, near this spot, will be begun, and that thus, ere long, another improvement will come into existence in Monmouth, and an additional facility afforded for our increasing road traffic.

But the assumption of a new bridge was unfounded. Led by the safety interests of Alderman A.H. Williams, the Town Council decided to approach the County Council to provide a second bridge on the grounds that many accidents were occurring there and that traffic congestion was becoming too great. It was said that thousands of pounds were being spent elsewhere in the county, yet, again, not a penny was being spent in the Monmouth district. No bridge was forthcoming. Thus, in 1928, the Town Council was persuaded by Councillor E.T.A. Williams that it was hopeless to ask the County once more. It was resolved that a deputation be sent to London to petition the Ministry of Transport for their intervention.[102]

In the 1930s Monmouth continued to ask for a bridge to relieve the ancient crossing. A viable relief bridge design was suggested by Mr O. Steen of Church Street in September 1931. Since the houses south of Monnow Bridge were no more, it would be simple to double the road width and to erect a single carriageway bridge adjacent to the old one. With new building techniques and materials it would be straightforward to throw a single span reinforced concrete bridge over the Monnow immediately downstream of the bridge (Fig. 43). The new bridge could be modern and yet complementary to the old structure. And, the old bridge could be preserved without alteration. But, despite such plans, no bridge appeared. Sir Joseph Bradney, the antiquarian, JP, and sometime alderman, laid blame at the door of socialists in the County Council. Although some progress had been made, including purchase and destruction of the cottages, in the spring of 1928 the socialists won a powerful majority. According to Bradney, Monnow Bridge was soon forgotten whilst grandiose and unnecessary schemes were undertaken elsewhere in the county. In defence of the County, Councillor Leonard Twiston-Davies pointed out that the County Council were wholly sympathetic to the unsatisfactory situation at the bridge. However, considering the then state of the country's finances, no relief bridge could be provided unless the County Surveyor could certify the ancient bridge as unsafe. He was unable so to do.[103]

Fig. 43. Elevation drawing for a proposed bridge alongside Monnow Bridge, each bridge to have one-way traffic.

Monnow Bridge carried the A40 trunk road at this time, the bridge being the only crossing of the Monnow from Overmonnow except for a foot-bridge at Beech Road and the two bridges from the Vauxhall fields. An A40 bypass road and bridge were seriously considered first in 1941. Such a bypass across Chippenham Mead and a river crossing would both relieve the town of through traffic and virtually eliminate congestion at the old bridge and Monnow Street. The plan ran into opposition due to finance and since the bypass road would require considerable destruction of buildings in order to take the new road from Wye Bridge on up to the existing Monmouth–Ross road at Dixton. A more radical bypass plan was considered also. In this second proposal a bridge would be built near the Troy railway bridges, and a second one over the Wye near Dixton, with a new roadway linking these to each other and the existing A40. This scheme might have worked well, causing minimal destruction, leaving Granville Street and Monmouth School untouched, and relieving Monnow Bridge of through traffic. However, the expense of two new bridges would have been considerable. Furthermore, this more distant bypass could have isolated Monmouth, encouraging few to visit, see the attractions, and assist cash flow. A meeting on site in June 1941 (involving the Ministry of Transport divisional engineer, the County Roads and Bridges Committee chairman, Sir Leonard Twiston-Davies, the County Surveyor, the Town Clerk, and several town councillors) resulted in a resolution to begin on the bypass via Chippenham Mead and Beech Road. The Ministry of War Transport agreed to pay one hundred per cent of the cost of a new bridge.[104]

The Monmouth bypass road and relief Monnow Bridge were built after some delays. As foreseen, the road bisected the Mead, replaced Granville Street and much of Old Dixton Road, and resulted later in congestion and many serious collisions at the junction with Wye Bridge. But, traffic was lessened dramatically at Monnow Bridge, at least for a while. With through traffic using the A40, Monnow Bridge (demoted to road B4293) was left to carry local traffic, buses, and delivery vehicles. But, as road traffic increased everywhere, so too did local traffic, with continuing collisions and congestion.

In 1981 the call for another new Monnow Bridge appeared, this time in the Monmouth Town Centre Plan Review. The document was prepared by Monmouth District Council, proposing a planning framework to guide and control development in Monmouth town centre. Traffic profiles are given for strategic points around the town, including Monnow Bridge. The figures, dating from monitoring in 1976 and 1978, show that, despite the bridge's use primarily for local traffic, the number of vehicles crossing per hour was becoming a considerable problem. In August 1976, between 9.00 a.m. and 6.00 p.m. figures varied between 649 and 800 vehicles per hour. At between 5.00 and 6.00 p.m. over 700 vehicles crossed. The standard theoretical traffic capacity of a six metre wide urban road was defined as 1,000 vehicles per hour. At the bridge the theoretical capacity would be 800 vehicles. A further measure of potential to carry traffic is the environmental capacity, which is defined as the capacity of a street to accommodate moving and stationary vehicles having regard to the need to maintain environmental standards. The environmental road capacity was calculated to be 392 vehicles per hour. The report's view of future traffic flow trends predicts rates far beyond the 1976 figures. As early as 1987 both the theoretical and environmental capacities were being exceeded. In July of that year analysed automatic traffic counts showed an average of 927 vehicles per hour between 5.00 and 6.00 p.m. on weekdays with an average of 10,131 vehicles per twenty-four hour period. After comparing these traffic flows and the calculated theoretical capacities, it is not at all surprising that the District Council reconsidered the bridge's future. The council proposed that 'a new road bridge shall be constructed over the River Monnow to replace Monnow Bridge', that the 'existing Monnow Bridge will be totally pedestrianised ... and the Monnow Bridge will be maintained as an Ancient Monument.' Optimistically, it was anticipated that design work would proceed and that construction would be in hand by the end of the plan's term in 1991.[105]

By the latter half of the 1980s public pressure began to push for some sign that design and construction would proceed. Most vociferous of the public was Monmouth Action Group, a conservation group whose first and most important campaign was towards 'saving' Monnow Bridge. In February 1986 officers of the Group presented a petition supported by 2,700 signatures asking the County to pedestrianize the old bridge, Cadw to 'restore' it, and the County to build the promised new bridge. The Highways Committee agreed to act on the proposals. However, later, the Highways Committee proclaimed that although they were fully aware of the problems at the bridge, there were 'insufficient funds available to provide a new bridge for some time' – a reason echoing words of the 1920s.[106]

The offer of a replacement bridge at no cost to the ratepayer has come several times, usually from development companies. Although fanfared in the Press, not all of these proposals actually resulted in formal representations to the authorities controlling the area. A chartered surveyor acting for Land Use Investments Ltd. made one such proposal in 1986. The proposed bridge would be built with a two-way road linking Monnow Street to Cinderhill Street, the extension of parking facilities at Chippenham, the creation of 150–200 additional jobs, and resiting of the 'unsightly' cattle market to the periphery of town. These improvements would accompany development of the old cattle market as a superstore, a frozen food outlet, and four other shops amounting to some 40,800 sq.ft. in all. This development would have changed the townscape of lower Monnow Street, restoring the cattle market area and riverside to a built-up area not seen there for decades.

A further and very similar free bridge offer came in 1989 from an estate agent representing civil engineers Kenneth Needs. Again, this scheme offered a bridge in return for an opportunity to develop the cattle market site. Most of these ideas have been supermarket based, involving a massively-scaled shop and equally massively-scaled parking areas, both of which conflict with the Borough Council's current philosophy for the bridge's vicinity. The bridge and surrounds are an integral part of the town's conservation area. In the event that the livestock market should move in the future to some other site, then it is probable that the construction of a mix of small-scale shops and housing would be encouraged rather than a scheme encompassing large outlets and vast areas of parking space. However, in 1992 Monmouth Borough Council granted planning permission for the erection of a Waitrose supermarket behind Monnow Street and on the site of a nearby disused council depot; a development which would not affect the cattle market or bridge vicinity and would not encompass any new bridge.[107]

The District Council applied some pressure towards provision of a new bridge for the economic well-being of the town, to enhance the tourism potential, and to protect the monument from further damage. Yet again, though, lack of finance was blamed for refusal by the County. However, the County's response was interpreted as a statement of intent in that they agreed the merit in proceeding with the design stage and at least bidding for the necessary capital allocation. Applications to Cadw and the EEC for grants were a possibility, but both were not effected. Cadw was not approached since its limited grant-aid was for the care of monuments, not to assist in building new bridges and roads. Euro-MP for south-east Wales, Llew Smith, spoke to the Action Group regarding EEC funding. As only one appropriate grant was given annually following two to three hundred UK applications, the chances of a successful Gwent County application would be slim indeed.[108]

For the following years the question of a replacement bridge ground on, frequently returning to the public forum in some guise. The protagonists remained Gwent County Council, Monmouth Borough Council, Monmouth Town Council, Monmouth Action Group, Cadw, various individuals, and a new group formed in 1989, the Friends of Monnow Bridge. At the end of 1987 the County Highways Committee made an assurance that the construction of another bridge was amongst 'possible starts for 1990/91 and beyond'. In response to enquiries from the Town Council, the County Engineer, M.S. Owen, stated that the ancient bridge could be closed to traffic to protect it, etc., but the situation with respect to a new bridge remained unchanged. No new bridge could be foreseen in the near future. Thus was raised an untenable proposition. The County could close the bridge in the short term to preserve and protect it, yet this would not coincide with erection of a replacement structure.[109]

By the close of 1989 the County Engineer wrote to Monmouth Town Council that he hoped to begin new bridge design procedures in 1990. Although no finance had yet been committed to enact the works, at least once the design phase was complete the County could proceed following the provision of sufficient funding. A new Structure Plan prepared by the County in 1991 only gave a commitment for a new bridge prior to the year 2006. However, during July 1991 topographical and geotechnical surveys were made in advance of design work for the new bridge, allowing a possible start date of 1993/94, subsequently revised to 'advance works and a scheme start' in 1994/95. Later in 1991, Cadw reiterated its view that the bridge's 'continued use as a busy modern road is difficult to reconcile with the need to preserve an ancient monument of such importance'.[110]

Monnow Bridge as a Symbol

Increasingly since the 1700s Monnow Bridge and Gate have become both unique and well known. They have been interpreted in souvenirs and art works. They have become symbols of Welsh tourism and Monmouth itself. And, their image has been adopted by local businesses and organizations.

Monnow Bridge's fame and singular character, taken with its intact condition and the absence of structures of equal stature nearby, have led to the monument becoming synonymous with the town and county. Anyone aware of Monmouth is aware of the peculiar bridge, much as thought of Blackpool suggests its tower or Pisa suggests its leaning campanile. It is this immediate recognition and association which have led to the bridge's image being employed by a number of Monmouth organizations. In the nineteenth century the Higgins grocery firm, with shops in Monnow Street and St Thomas's Square, used an impressive steel engraving on their bags for the Overmonnow shop, depicting the street and Monnow Gate (Fig.

Fig. 44. An engraving of Overmonnow and Monnow Bridge from a paper bag of Higgins's Grocery Establishment. The pedestrians are rendered on a small scale probably to emphasize the grandeur of the buildings.

44). Here the bridge helps to orientate prospective customers. But, for many other concerns, a link with the bridge was made where no innate association existed. J.B. Hyam and C.N. Ballinger Ltd., late mineral water manufacturers of Glendower Street, employed Monnow Gate as their trademark, using a view of the building surrounded by the words PONT – MYNWY [Monnow Bridge] MONMOUTH. This appeared on their letterhead, and embossed upon earthenware and glass bottles. A similar view of the gate was taken by Monnow Catering as its device. An advertisement brochure produced by Bailey Homes Ltd. for their thirty retirement flats built in 1988 on a former orchard overlooking Chippenham Mead enjoyed a stylized colour drawing of the gate at the head of the front cover.

In 1942 H.M. Bateman, the cartoonist and caricaturist, drew a portfolio of sketches in support of Warship Week. In this cause communities were encouraged to give generously towards the provision of ships for the war effort. The regional Warship Week campaigns were intended actually to stimulate public loan investment to sponsor ships appropriate to the size of the community. Bateman's sketch for Monmouth and District (Fig. 45) is both innovative and a personal view for Monmouth. Here is the ubiquitous gate with the hopeful new ship ploughing through waves of cheques, coins, and banknotes. Monmouth responded well to the call, raising in total £110,516.8s.7d. when for a minesweeper the appeal target had been £62,000.[111]

Fig. 45. H.M. Bateman's Warship Week cartoon for Monmouth in 1942.

The annual agricultural Monmouthshire Show has repeatedly taken the gate for its publicity, using a stylized view for posters. Hugh Crowther drew a gate sketch, used for many years on the show's official programme of events. Crowther, a local artist who drew many local topographical scenes, also drew a large view for the background of a certificate of gratitude from the town to local Second World War veterans. This background portrays the modern bridge on which stands a medieval herald, a banner with the town armorial bearings, signatures of the three 1939–46 mayors, and a statement of gratitude to the soldier.[112]

In 1991 a stylized view of Monnow Gate became the main feature of the badge designed by the Monmouth branch of the Royal Naval Association to be used on the new HMS *Monmouth*, then under construction on the Clyde. The ship's senior officer, Cmdr. C.J. Holgate wrote congratulating the local branch on the design's acceptance by the Ministry of Defence. The ship joined the fleet in April 1993.[113]

Monnow Bridge has appeared prominently also in tourist and promotional literature produced by the Monmouth Chamber of Commerce, the Borough Council, the Wales Tourist Board, and the National Trust, none of which benefit directly from bridge tourists. But, the bridge's potential effect upon local cash flow is considerable. Thus, the bridge has appeared in association with numerous civic and business concerns, and the Borough Council and Chamber of Commerce have produced many thousands of envelopes and leaflets featuring the structure. 'An Old Trader' wrote to the *Beacon* in 1937 recommending that the Chamber should begin a campaign of press releases to spread the appreciation of Monmouth's assets. To accompany a photograph of Monnow Bridge to be sent to all national daily newspapers, he suggested the following enlightening caption.

The Monmouth Chamber of Trade strongly opposes, on historical grounds as against modern traffic needs, any proposal to destroy this ancient building which contains in its gateway many interesting records of its long history from the 13th century to Chartist times, when it was fortified against the Newport rioters.

Apparently, such newsworthy releases were not distributed. But, in 1952 came the suggestion that in fact the use of the bridge in the publicizing of Monmouth was being overdone. In reply, the Chamber of Commerce's president said that the bridge had been used a lot and 'he agreed that Monnow Bridge was the hallmark of Monmouth and that the Town was proud of it'.[114]

Other than adoption by the Chamber, the monument has featured in works of art, books, and souvenir objects. During the nineteenth century a wide range of engravings, lithographs, and etchings of Monnow Bridge were published in topographical works. Many unique works survive, some of which are important historical witnesses of the period, others of which are more a reflection of the artist's creativity. Paintings and drawings reproduced elsewhere in this book generally accurately portray the structure at a particular point. There are some, however, which give a portrayal as the building never was. John Crome's oil painting (Fig. 9) employs some artistic licence. Two other original works exist in stained glass. At Baron Llangattock's mansion, The Hendre, near Monmouth, the library has stained glass views including one of the bridge. Here, armoured medieval knights canter over the bridge and an Arthurian rowing boat glides underneath, complete with a pretty maiden. The bridge has a portcullis (in the wrong position), the chinaman's hat roof (of *c*.1706), and pedestrian passageways (by the 1850s). Perhaps the portcullis and figures had come to the bridge via a time warp! Another strange portrayal exists in the music room at Dinmore Manor, near Hereford. Here, though, although based upon Monnow Bridge, there has been no claim that this shows the structure as it used to be. The stained glass window (Fig. 46) takes as its subject the Canterbury Pilgrims, crossing over a stylized Monnow Bridge, with a background townscape suitable to the late fourteenth century. This attractive and brightly coloured work was made for the room (erected between 1932 and 1936) by Messrs W. Morris (Westminster) Ltd.[115]

Fig. 46. Monnow Bridge as an inspiration for a stained glass window of the Canterbury Pilgrims at Dinmore Manor.

Although no in-depth account of the bridge has been published, its uniqueness has produced short passages in works on bridges and medieval fortification. Amongst these have been A.J. Taylor's official guide to Monmouth Castle, Jervoise's *Ancient Bridges of Wales*, Mrs Bagnall-Oakeley's *Monnow Bridge Tower*, and Richards's *Book of Bridges*. Accounts have been generally superficial, with the above ones giving fuller accounts than most. The late Fred Hando published an inimitable bridge essay as one of his long series of popular articles for the *South Wales Argus*, later reprinted as parts of books in 1964 and 1989. His essay, enlightening to the general newspaper reader, is augmented by Hando's poetic licence. After awaiting a pause in traffic flow, apparently Hando unlocked the 'ancient' door and threaded himself 'up the spiral stone stairs and the steep wooden steps to the upper floor of the tower'. Hando does not date his visit, but the spiral stone steps have been absent since 1819. Nevertheless, his essay is informative and entertaining.[116]

The bridge has been interpreted also in souvenirs. Sundry mugs, dishes, pots, and tapestry patterns are available with images of the gate or bridge, and there has been, of course, a wide selection of photographic sepia and colour postcards since before 1900. But, other than these, several good quality sculptures and models have been available. At the beginning of this century, the first ones were very similar white glazed china models made by W.H. Goss and Co. (around 95 mm. and 103 mm. tall), Willow Potteries (around 92 mm. tall), and Savoy China (around 106 mm. and 112 mm. tall). These sometimes had colouring, though this was usually limited to gold highlights. When actually purchased in Monmouth, the Goss ones were available with the Monmouth town armorial bearings emblazoned over the roof. In the 1950s W.J. Barber of Llandogo produced hand-painted half relief models of the gate (105 mm. tall) for sale in Monmouth. More up to date, in 1988 was released a model produced locally by a firm called Helcon. Coming from a mould, the 120 mm. tall model in two-tone brown successfully resembles the monument; though none of these models approaches the detail and exceptional accuracy of Barber's creation.[117]

Monmouth Flood Alleviation Scheme

Monmouth has long been a site of flooding caused by the Monnow and Wye rivers and their local tributaries. Recent excavations under Monnow Street buildings have shown evidence of a number of major floods sufficient to leave individual layers of deposition in the strata. There are also what appear to be deliberately placed layers of household refuse and building materials, possibly laid in an effort to raise the ground level. Abandonment of many buildings along Monnow Street in the mid-fourteenth century had previously been attributed solely to the Black Death, which caused particular upheaval locally in 1348–9 and 1369. But, the presence of near contemporary siltation up Monnow Street to beyond the defensive ditch raises the possibility of abandonment due to excessive flooding. Evidence of very serious flooding as high up as 22–4 Monnow Street has been dated to approximately 1315–45. It is recorded that in

1348 there was rain every day from Easter until Christmas. This may correspond to the heavy siltation of up to eight inches depth from around that time. Modern flooding records reach back as far as 1795. These indicate that, although the Monnow and Wye flood fairly frequently, major flooding up Monnow Street and throughout Overmonnow occurs at an average of once in thirty years. The strength of Monnow floods is said to have lessened considerably in modern times when in 1856 the mouth of the river was realigned so that the Monnow enters the Wye at an acute angle rather than the old right-angled junction.[118]

By modern design standards Monnow Bridge has small, low river arches with a great deal of masonry as a potential water obstruction (Fig. 47). The impediment to flow when in flood can be seen when the water level approaches the tops of the bridge arches. Then there is a considerable drop in surface level as water passes under the bridge. The River Wye Catchment Board's General Report of 1933 summarized the problem, C.H.J. Clayton writing that

Monnow gate Bridge, although a charming antiquity, offers a serious obstruction to flow. It has 3 spans, but two only of them appear to be normally effective, the third being obstructed by a deep cess. As an instance of the obstructive character of this bridge, Mr. Biddle [W.J.H. Biddle, Monmouth Borough Surveyor] informed me that on the occasion of the 1929 flood the fall through the bridge spans was as much as 16 inches.

Fig. 47. Monnow Bridge viewed from downstream, August 1981.

In order to lessen Monmouth's flooding and the obstruction caused by Monnow Bridge, the report made a number of recommendations. These included clearing of river obstructions, regrading of the banks, widening of the channel above the bridge, and the construction of a flood bank to protect the lower part of the town from flooding. For the bridge itself, an unspecified modification to the structure was suggested.[119]

Not until fifty years after the Catchment Board Report did a comprehensive scheme begin to alleviate Monmouth flooding. It should be noted that this scheme, orchestrated by the Welsh Water Authority, was designed to alleviate flooding, not to eliminate it. The scheme encompassed such measures as flood embankments and reinforced walls at the top of the natural river banks, a pit to absorb local flooding from tributaries, flood gates, and fixtures to prevent river water from entering surface water drains. By these means the strategy was followed of flood alleviation via containment of the two rivers within their natural courses. If successful, then on all but the most severe flood occasions the rivers would remain contained. Any flooding would be from small tributaries rather than from the rivers.

The bridge, through its solid, antiquated design, already presented a formidable obstacle to water flow. If under conditions that formerly would have caused major flooding the river is forced to keep within its heightened banks, then the situation occurs of an irresistible (?) force pressing on an immovable (?) object. Hence, as part of the flood alleviation scheme, investigations were made and works were effected to reinforce the stability of the bridge.

In August 1983 a small concrete apron was laid at bed level around the northern quarter of the tower pier. But, rather than being the beginning of flood scheme works, this apron was an independent maintenance measure taken by the County Council to protect against scour. Preparations for the flood scheme proper began in 1983 and 1984 when site investigations were conducted at the bridge. In order to identify the river bed make-up and the depth of any solid substrate, eight trial pits were excavated into the bed, three upstream and five downstream of the bridge. Six much deeper samples (down to 4.25 m. below the bed level) were taken via boreholes. The excavations and cores revealed a highly variable bed of gravel, sand, and silt over clay mudstone (marl). As one would expect, the amount and type of loose material over the marl varied according to each sample's position in the river channel. Marl varied between 0.05 m. and 2.7 m. below water surface level, with water depths of 0.05 m. to 1.2 m. The bed profiles gained from these samples were useful in planning the later works.[120]

At the same time that the bed samples were taken, four holes were bored into the piers, three into the tower pier and one into pier two. Since two of these were horizontal and two directed downward at 42° and 45° angles, the cores obtained allowed some analysis of the pier interiors and the nature of any pier foundations. The horizontal cores showed as expected that the sandstone block exterior (to a depth of 0.35 m.) surrounds a core of sandstone rubble and cement. The raked cores passed through the ashlar work and the rubble. This core material continues down lower than the exterior stonework. Lower still, bore one encountered a timber beam apparently 0.55 m. thick. This rested upon 1.05 m. of gravel over the mudstone substrate, which continued down at least to the full bore depth of 4.80 m. and 4.50 m. The borehole samples did not reveal the significance of the massive timber structure far beneath the visible pier. The wood could have represented a random block of discarded building material thrown into the infill, part of a timber raft pier foundation, part of a timber pile foundation, or even some remnant of an earlier wooden bridge. Fortuitously, the answer came during the ensuing flood scheme works in 1988.[121]

The Monmouth Flood Alleviation Scheme was effected in 1988 to 1990 by Alfred McAlpine Construction with Sir William Halcrow and Partners as engineers, the client being the Welsh Water Authority. That part which directly affected Monnow Bridge was the construction of a reinforced concrete slab across the full width of the river channel underneath the bridge. The purpose was to stabilize the bridge foundations and the surrounding river bed, and to prevent bed scouring which might lead to undermining of the piers. Although requiring massive machinery and considerable force, the slab design and procedures employed were simple and efficient, involving sheet piles bordering slabs of reinforced concrete. Prior to large scale pile-driving, tell-tales were attached across already existing cracks in walls within the gate along with metal studs at cracks within and without. Thus, engineers were able to detect and monitor any negative structural effects resulting from nearby works. Piling vibration tests were made on a Sunday with the bridge closed to vehicles. As the pile-driving machine drove sheet piles into the river bed, a meter was employed to measure vibration at several locations on the bridge, closely observed by the project resident engineer, C.D. James, and Welsh Water representatives. Pile-driving proceeded as planned when the vibrations being created proved to be well below that caused by normal bridge traffic.[122]

Throughout October 1988 two walls of steel sheet piles were erected, with each pile being driven as far as possible into the river bed. After each of the six wall sections had been driven in, a dam was built around the section, and, whilst water was pumped out, the piles were cut off at the nominal river bed level (Fig. 48). The operation left two metal walls extending down from bed level into rock and crossing the Monnow a little above and below the piers. The next phase was to excavate out the river bed, one span at a time, below the bridge, so that at least 450 mm. of space was exposed below the top of the pile walls. As originally planned, the artificial bed between the pile walls was constructed of a gravel drainage layer, a polythene separation sheet, and 300 mm. of reinforced concrete. Coloured to blend with the sandstone bridge masonry, the resulting artificial bed is a firm, smooth surface, strengthening bridge stability and streamlining water flow.[123]

During excavations prior to laying the reinforced concrete slab, a number of items and much information were revealed from the bridge's past. As little was known of the bridge pier foundations and the depth of ashlar masonry, exploratory excavations were necessary before work could proceed adjacent to the abutments or piers. At the Monmouth arch a build-up of silt required digging out before even the nominal river bed level was reached. At the

Fig. 48. Monmouth flood alleviation scheme. Piles being cut off, on 20 October 1988, prior to construction of the river bed protection slab under Monnow Bridge.

Monmouth abutment the medieval builders evidently had anticipated silt build-up, perhaps based upon experience with the previous wooden bridge. Here the ashlar masonry ends much higher than at the pier faces surrounded by water (Fig. 49). Below is tidy masonry, but not of ashlar quality, down to well below nominal water level. Excavation at the northern face of the tower pier uncovered the concrete shoulder of 1983. An excavation at the south end of that pier on 28 October uncovered the unexpected – a massive timber structure extending out from under the tower pier at a level well below the water level.[124]

On 2–4 November 1988 the Glamorgan-Gwent Archaeological Trust carried out an excavation and recording of the timber structures beneath the tower pier led by archaeologist C.N. Maylan. Just under the lowest part of the ashlar pier masonry a stout vertical timber runs down to, and is jointed into, an horizontal timber which runs in beneath the pier (Fig. 50). Just before this 'sole plate' recedes into the rubble masonry, a smaller transverse timber rises off the plate, vanishing also into the masonry. The arrangement of these timbers is unlikely to have been made as a·pier foundation for the existing bridge. The position of the pieces coincides neither with the expected configuration for a timber raft foundation nor for that of timber piles. Instead, the arrangement is typical of medieval trestle-type wooden bridges. Such bridges had heavy wooden trestles standing on the river bed with their long axes parallel with water flow to lessen the water

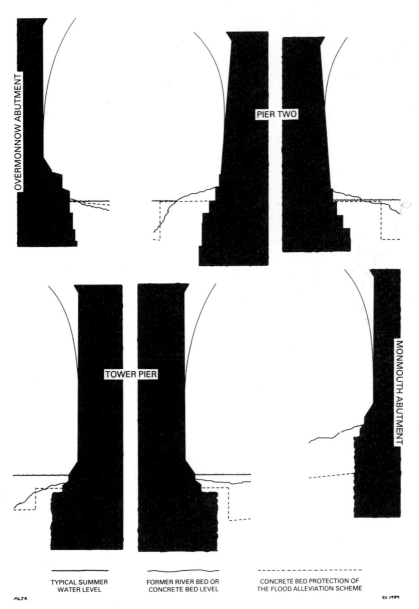

TYPICAL SUMMER
WATER LEVEL

FORMER RIVER BED OR
CONCRETE BED LEVEL

CONCRETE BED PROTECTION OF
THE FLOOD ALLEVIATION SCHEME

Fig. 49. Profile drawings of the bridge piers and abutments at the time of the flood alleviation works, indicating typical water surface level, the bed protection slab of the flood alleviation scheme, and the previous bed.

Fig. 50. Foundations of the tower pier that were found under the eastern face of the downstream cutwater, photographed (3 November 1988) after the end of the sole plate had been removed for analysis. The metal beam is part of the shuttering used during the excavation.

pressure. A flat wooden deck would have been carried bank-to-bank over the series of trestles. Although such trestles had numerous individual designs, common to these are vertical timbers and transverse bracing struts jointed into massive recumbent sole plates. This leads to the suggestion that these timbers at the bridge are the cut off or ruined remains of a wooden bridge pre-dating the present stone Monnow Bridge. If so, then this discovery is particularly important since archaeological evidence has been recorded of few medieval wooden bridges from the midst of rivers. Most similar surviving remains examined in modern times have been found in the tranquil depths of moated sites.[125]

After recording the exposed timber remains, the archaeologists removed a 12.5 cm. slice from the end of the sole plate for analysis. Throughout the entire dig the wood was kept saturated with water to prevent deterioration. Once the Trust had completed its work, the engineers and contractors proceeded with a modified collar construction around the tower pier base so that the wooden remains could remain saturated. With the pier collar complete on the north-east side, work began to excavate out the bed between the tower pier and the Monmouth abutment. Only days after the initial discoveries, further and greater evidence of the previous wooden bridge was found. In the midst of the Monmouth span river bed was found a further complete bridge sole plate. Eight metres long, the sole plate was orientated, as was the first one, for a bridge almost exactly on the same site as the existing one. The cut off remains of three upright timbers and several transverse struts survived, attached as before by mortise and tenon joints. Further samples were taken for dating, as well as some timber intended for treatment and exhibition. However, after being suitably protected, the entire sole plate was entombed within the new bed protection slab.[126]

Dating of the timber bridge remains was carried out by dendrochronological analysis. Within a geographical region the pattern of annual growth rings in trees of the same species will be comparable, creating statistically similar ring patterns. Since records of these patterns have been pieced together, sometimes reaching back over thousands of years, good samples of ancient timber can be dated often with precision. The samples of oak from Monnow Bridge were analysed by Dr Ruth Morgan of Sheffield University, funded by Halcrow. Between the samples Morgan found matching of rings and good comparison to dated tree samples from the south and west of England. Little trace of sapwood remained on the samples, as one might expect from timber prepared for building use. This lack prevented a precise felling date, forcing the date given to be bracketed. Bearing in mind an allowance for sapwood, Morgan concluded that the timber had been felled sometime between AD 1123 and 1169. This gives a construction date of up to around 1180. Destruction of the bridge may have occurred, as outlined earlier, in the 1233 Battle of Monmouth, during the lordship of John of Monmouth.[127]

Throughout the rest of the bed protection works at Monnow Bridge few other archaeological artefacts were discovered other than the decayed fragment of a rifle, numerous bullets, and fragments of pottery and glassware. This lack of further significant discoveries was due mainly to the extensive works carried out in 1892. It will be recalled that in that year the central and Overmonnow spans were each dammed and excavated out. The raked out river bed was then largely covered with concrete and much of pier two was refaced down to a considerable depth. Other than the finds of 1892 already discussed, no records mention finding timber structural remains at that time. Possibly any further remains of a timber bridge were lost before 1892, or they were destroyed then and not recorded. During the modern flood scheme, the rough Victorian concrete was removed from around the piers and the abutments. However, for much of the bed beneath the middle and Overmonnow spans, the old concrete was sufficiently low that the new bed protection could proceed without removing the old work. Thus, it is possible that the bridge remains are *in situ* to this day, beneath the Victorian bed works.[128]

Monmouth flood alleviation scheme was completed in 1990. But, a test of its efficacy came several months *before* its completion. At the end of January 1990, persistent heavy rain swelled the two rivers and the tributaries at Monmouth (Fig. 51). Both rivers were contained where required, preventing river flooding into Monnow Street and Overmonnow. But, flooding did occur in Chippenham Mead and at Overmonnow as a result of overflows of the streams in Watery Lane and Wonastow Road. Minor adjustments to the flood scheme measures were called for to lessen these tributary flooding effects.[129]

Fig. 51. Monnow Gate viewed from the south-south-west on 28 January 1990, during flood conditions.

Maintenance and Conservation

Except for the massive repair programme in the 1890s, and a conservation project during autumn 1989, records produce little evidence of major maintenance works in the past century. This could be due to the considerable obstacles that the roadway and the river present to the the access of workmen, and partly to the requirement of maintaining free traffic flow.

To assist in protecting the structure, vehicle height and weight restrictions were adopted. Prior to the Second World War large vehicles did cross the bridge, but it was not until mid-1940 that the County Surveyor suggested that it would be desirable to restrict larger vehicles. HM Office of Works agreed, and the County Roads and Bridges Committee recommended that Section 46(2) of the Road Traffic Act 1930, as amended by Section 29 of the Road and Rail Traffic Act 1933, be put into operation. During 1946 came into effect the 1944 County Council of Monmouthshire Roads (Restriction) Order with the placement of traffic restriction warnings at the approaches to the town. However, later the Chamber of Commerce and the Town Council campaigned for a change to the order. Their complaint was that the wording of the signs was misleading some motorists into believing that the bridge was closed to all vehicles. Thus, many prospective visitors to the town supposedly bypassed it. In 1955 a new order reduced the length of restricted road, the wording of the signs, and their placement. The signs close to the bridge read 'Prohibited. Locomotives, tractors, heavy motor cars with seats for more than eight persons, except single deck buses'. It was not until later that the 10 ft. 3 in. advisory headroom restriction was added, and the weight restriction was made more precise at three tons unladen in 1966. In the fifteen years to 1990 the restriction signs changed in size and position. When such signs are inconspicuous or unclear it is not surprising that large and heavy vehicles cross the bridge which strictly are prohibited. But, even when signs are explicit and obvious, enforcement of the restrictions is difficult.[130]

Evidence of plans for comprehensive maintenance works appear in the form of an elevation drawing of the bridge dated 5 August 1942. Prepared by the Ministry of Transport, the drawing indicates scaffolding to cocoon the entire bridge and gate, including instructions for the placement of platforms. However, no written reports survive to indicate that such exhaustive works ever took place.[131]

In June of 1956 the Ministry of Works wrote to the County Council regarding repair works which it considered essential at Monnow Gate. The County Surveyor was able to report to committee that the repair costs, estimated at £550, were available, and, in addition, the Ministry of Transport was prepared to offer a seventy-five per cent grant towards the costs. In due course the works to the gate's south-west arch proceeded, resulting in closure of the bridge to all traffic except for service buses.[132]

Only a year later, calls for more exhaustive repairs at the gate came from the Monmouthshire Local History Council and the Monmouth and District Chamber of Commerce. Their comments were that the bridge was in a bad state of repair and disintegrating bit by bit. 'If we are not careful it might become a total loss', commented Mr Hector Lee at a Chamber of Commerce meeting. Conservation works at the tower began in September, continuing through the autumn. The *Beacon* reported that this was the 'first full "facial" for about 30 years.' In November some matching 'new' stone was employed, reused from a demolished stable and barn at Whitebrook.[133]

The 1957 maintenance works were wholly cosmetic, mostly involving pointing of the masonry and making good of some decaying stones. No noticeable changes occurred to the road arches or to any of the principal design features. However, it appears to be during these works that the prominent hole and projecting stone high over the downstream pedestrian arch were obliterated. These features were an original part of the gate's ancient design, acting as a rain-water drain for the wall-walk (Figs. 29, 30, 31, and 35). Photographs of Monnow Gate indicate the drain to be intact in September 1955 yet destroyed by May 1958. Perhaps unaware of its significance, the 1957 masons sliced off the projecting spout and filled the accompanying drain hole.[134]

Claims have been made that cleaning and maintenance of the gate interior have been largely neglected by the responsible authority. In 1963 the local Chamber of Commerce noted the neglected condition and resolved to ask the County Council to carry out cleaning of the gate and the C.S. Rolls memorial statue in Agincourt Square. Members of the Monmouth Round Table took matters into their own hands in 1972, removing pigeon droppings and tidying up the tower room. The situation had deteriorated again by 1980 when again the Chamber of Commerce expressed dissatisfaction with the apparent lack of maintenance at the bridge. Conrad Hughes, a Chamber member, said that 'tourism was all important to the town and it seemed wrong that one of the things people came to see – the bridge – was "being neglected". There seemed to be no maintenance carried out on the bridge and ... if the authorities were not able to do anything then ... Chamber members could "spruce it up a bit" themselves.' Another letter to the County Council was ordered.[135]

Taking cleaning duties into their own hands was suggested yet again in 1990, this time by the Monmouth Action Group. The condition of the bridge frequently entering their agendas, the filthy state of the gate room and the furnishings led members to agree to a spring-clean of their own. But, by 1992 entry of pigeons via the musket holes had resulted in another good layer of droppings on all horizontal surfaces.

Besides being dirty, the furnishings had been allowed also to decay to the point of falling apart. The two Bagnall-Oakeley water-colours and the murage grant transcript had been removed. This left the two pictures presented by Sir Henry Mather-Jackson in 1926, and the furniture presented in 1902. Although basically sound, by 1989 the chair upholstery had perished and hardware on the table had decayed to such an extent that the leaves had fallen off. The suggestion was made to the County Council that, since they own the building, and, presumably, its contents, they ought to make some effort to repair and preserve the furnishings. Instead, that authority passed responsibility to the Town Council. Since the Town Council 'had shown a keen interest in the bridge', the County suggested that 'they might like to launch an appeal for the renovation of the table and chair'. The furnishings were not repaired.[136]

The 'deplorable state' of Monnow Bridge was discussed in Town Council and Chamber of Commerce meetings in May 1978. Councillor George Butler pointed out that there was damage to both road arches, the archway ceiling was ripped, and the ceiling mouldings were gradually falling off. He believed that if the bridge was not maintained properly 'it will not be long before it is not Monnow Bridge people will be coming to see, it will be the ruins of Monnow Bridge'. In the two meetings complaints were made also that a window was broken, the tower room was filthy, and the gate key was lodged at some locality unknown to any of them present. The suggestion was made of reinstating the portcullis, *and* the winding gear, to make the bridge an even greater asset to the town. In due course, the Town Clerk wrote to the County Council regarding these observations. The County Council closed the road for a day at the beginning of June. Remedial work was carried out on the ceiling, whilst several arch stones were replaced but not a portcullis.[137]

Between 1978 and 1989 no significant maintenance works occurred beyond the major repair programmes required in 1982 and 1985 as described earlier. Miscellaneous minor works included the replacement of slipped tilestones on the roof, window repairs, and the laying of new road and footpath paving.

Five glazed windows existed at the gate: the large round-headed window facing Monnow Street, the square leaded window over the wooden stairway, the leaded 'attic' window facing St Thomas's Square, and glass in the two plain arrow slits (Fig. 72). The latter three were first glazed during the 1890's restoration. By 1986 the glass of the plain arrow slit at the garderobe passage had been smashed, the square window over the stairway lay in a mutilated heap on the floor with nineteen of the sixty panes broken (hence the ingress of birds and their droppings), and the large round-headed window was virtually unopenable. Brought to the attention of the County Council, with input from Cadw, the square window was restored superbly and returned to its position overlooking the cattle market. The arrow slit glazing repair was omitted. Historically no glass would have filled the arrow slits. The Victorians glazed the plain slits not as a restoration but to exclude the elements. Thus, it was not considered proper to restore this modern feature.

Footpath paving over the bridge has been replaced on several occasions in modern times. The County Council paved the footpaths with flagstones in 1889. In front of the gate the paths were bound by kerbstones. Behind, metal kerbing was used. In 1955 the by then parlous paving was relaid with concrete flags. No record remains of any significant re-laying between these dates. Beginning in 1985, a project began of replacing paving completely throughout the town centre with grey geometrical interlocking bricks. Monnow Bridge was not spared from this scheme; in the summer of 1985 the downstream pavement was replaced, and in December the upstream path was done. Since utility pipes lay directly under the paving, the change to bricks caused a noticeable increase in footpath surface height. At the same time new stone kerbing was installed, and covering of the road with up to two inches of asphalt (February 1988) lessened the apparent path height change. Although this brick paving may be easier to maintain than flagstones, it is questionable in at least this instance whether or not it is appropriate to employ modern bricks of abstract shape when elsewhere on the ancient monument traditional materials exist throughout. New genuine stone flags may have been the preferred paving material.[138]

The largest and most successful maintenance programme at Monnow Gate for almost a century occurred in the autumn of 1989. Gwent County Council officers conducted a survey of Monnow Gate on 5 June 1988. As the roadway was closed to traffic for the event, an hydraulic platform was employed to observe every square inch of the exterior from the roadway up to the roof's ridge tiles. The less than sound state of the road arches was obvious from ground level. However, the versatility of the platform allowed measurement and examination of features that are rarely accessible. The gate inspection resulted in the preparation of a Monnow Bridge Gatehouse Condition Report which summarized the condition and made recommendations for repair works. The main imperfections included a displaced arch ring, cracked masonry, and severely eroded stonework. After consultations with Cadw, a programme of repairs was undertaken in October and November 1989.[139]

Under specifications detailed by the County Engineer, the works were carried out by Stonewest Cox Ltd. of Newport. Estimates for the cost of the works ranged between £25,000 and £30,000. In such works the unnecessary alteration of design or replacement of historic fabric can seriously undermine the value or authenticity of an historic building. Clearly, in these works at Monnow Gate, some new stonework was going to be unavoidable. Thus, a search was made for quality stone which would match that existing on the gate. Following information from a local geologist and the Monmouth Action Group, a local quarry was investigated from which stone for the gate is likely to have come previously. However, much expense would have been entailed in reopening the quarry, and there was no guarantee that new stone from that source would be both workable and of sufficient quality. Eventually, similar red sandstone from Hollington, Staffordshire, was selected and approved for use by Gwent County and Cadw. To reflect the mixture of stone types now present on the gate, the Hollington stone was supplemented in these works by grey Forest of Dean sandstone.[140]

The stone lintel at the south end of the downstream pedestrian passage, which had been cracked for several decades, received treatment. The main tower room window was removed completely for specialist repairs. All timber was treated with a spray-applied permethrin-based compound, and a floor-board was raised to allow treatment within the floor/ceiling.[141]

Within the road passage of the gate both side walls contained eroded masonry requiring attention, particularly on the south side. Over much of this area, and below the door, the depth of this damage was so great that a plastic repair was impractical (Fig. 66). Thus, the face was replaced largely with new stone, few of the old stones being good enough for reuse. At the door a new jamb stone was inserted at the bottom left, and a new door sill, both in grey sandstone. At the same time the opportunity was taken to remove and rehang the door as the hinges had shifted from their original placement.

Stone replacement at road level on the south-west façade downstream led to some public disapproval. Adjacent to the wall repairs just noted is the portcullis chase, in front of which were three large very heavily eroded stones extending up from the road. These were replaced by large grey sandstone blocks, shaped to retain the portcullis groove. In addition to being called 'a horrible mess' and 'diabolical', two complaints were levelled subsequently: the stones 'stick out like a sore thumb' since they resemble two blocks of concrete, and, they are inappropriate since they project proud of the adjacent old stonework. The answer to the first complaint is that grey sandstone and Hollington red stone had been approved for these works, and in this instance the masons chose grey stone. Had the red stone been used, then perhaps the new stone would not have been so apparent. In fact, none of the three removed eroded blocks were noticeably of red stone. All were quite pale; the top one having a rich, golden colour. Regarding the latter complaint, the masons were on much firmer ground. Although it is true that now the new blocks project further than the stones directly above, the faces of the new stones are in alignment with the wall faces in both planes. There are fundamental principles when replacing facing stones on ancient buildings that

(a) there should be replacement only where essential, and (b) the faces of the new stones should align *with the original wall faces*. Setting of the new stones to line up with surrounding stones that have weathered is strenuously avoided. If a building composed of soft stone is restored against this rule, then, ultimately, the building will shrink because all new replacement stones have been set to align with adjacent stones rather than the original face. Both stones at the gate were placed in the proper position. The surviving eroded stones above simply emphasize placement of the new stones along the original wall face.[142]

Over several areas of Monnow Gate, pointing was carried out along surface cracks. In the downstream pedestrian passage preparation for this pointing revealed part of the original gate wall interior. When this passage was created the downstream wall of the tower curved around at this point, as it does above the passage. In order to make a flat downstream side wall for the passage, a mixture of stone and brick was used to fill the concave void. Prior to repointing here in 1989, loose mortar was raked out down to solid. This operation exposed two vertical chasms in the wall showing smooth stone faces going into the wall. This, of course, was the covered up inner face of the gate's curved original wall.

Although the main job of the 1989 conservation works was the rebuilding of the south-west road arch, the north-east arch required work also. Two voussoirs of that arch had been damaged by collisions, and adjacent to these, a small area of weathered stone had to be attended to. Thus, the archway was given support whilst arch stones were removed from the eleven o'clock position (facing south-west). Two voussoirs were replaced with Hollington stone when the stones were reinserted. This stone was employed also to reface the weathered area directly above.

Rebuilding of the perenially damaged south-west road arch was the main task of this works programme. The resulting new arch was undoubtedly an improvement over that erected in 1982. However, compromises were forced upon the work to ensure structural integrity. The main reason to rebuild the arch was that it had become potentially unsafe. No doubt as a result of vehicles, the arch ring had been displaced forward, causing some separation of the faces of the wall above, and cracking in that wall.

Although the south-west arch at Monnow Gate is likely to have been a segmental gothic arch in ancient times, for centuries the arch has been semicircular, and it would be wrong to restore it back to some ancient idealized point. Such a restoration would constitute a forgery that would ignore the centuries of life and numerous small modifications that the gate has seen. Instead, unless known conservation errors have occurred in the recent past, it is better to replace like with like, though preferably not creating a situation in which a modern restoration could be confused with original work. To this end a wooden centring was built with a diameter equal to the distance between the road passage side walls. In theory this could be raised up under the old arch and then temporarily fixed in place. However, this procedure was confounded. The four old arch springing stones stick out from the side walls at sharp angles, and the 1982 arch between them was noticeably askew. Thus, unfortunately, unable to raise the centring into position, the contractor had to remove the old arch totally, all at one time. Support of the wall above was afforded via scaffolding whilst the arch and spandrel wall was dismantled up to just underneath the machicolation corbels. This left a clear space in which the new arch could be built easily, and then the wall above could be filled in.[143]

Voussoirs for the new arch were cut specifically to fit the semicircular shape at the gate. In an effort to reflect the mixture of stone types present before the 1982 repairs, the twenty-one new stones were mixed: red Hollington, and grey Forest of Dean stone. At each side of the new arch the two original springing stones were to be retained. Thus, the new arch consisted of twenty-five voussoirs. Rather than the set of identical rather small arch stones of 1982, the new stones varied slightly in the circumferential dimension; their size being bolder, more akin to the four massive springers. To match the old voussoirs a chamfer was cut at the front bottom of each new stone. Although initially the rebate at the back edge was to be omitted, examination of historical evidence, such as the John Carter drawings (Fig. 17), showed that indeed the original arch was rebated to accept the now long-lost doors.[144]

The second change of plans in the 1989 programme involved the diameter of the arch itself. The new voussoirs were prepared specifically for an arch which, like the north-east road arch, would have an inside diameter equal to the distance between the two arch side walls. At the south-west, to make such an arch that would spring from the walls smoothly would require setting back some of the four springing arch stones into the side walls. *In situ* the four stones did not allow a smooth junction. Old illustrations show that the reason for the roughly projecting springing stones was not that they had been placed in the wrong position recently, but originally the arch rose off stone jambs which projected from the side walls. Thus, below the arch, on each side, jambs projected by about 5½ inches. Like the arch stones, the front of the jambs had a chamfer. As the jamb rose from the road, at the arch springing point the front chamfer continued around the arch and the back of the jambs continued as a 5½ in. deep rebate behind the arch. One of the old springing stones on the upstream side is a little misleading since in its present condition it implies that the arch chamfer tapers away to nothing as the arch meets the wall. But, originally this was clearly not the case. In the nineteenth century the jambs were removed to give extra road width, and the four springing stones were spared but partly mutilated. Thus, bearing in mind the former jambs, the re-created road arch should have an inside diameter equal to the distance between the road side walls *minus* about 11 in., giving a diameter of around 129 in. Ideally the rebuilt arch should have been constructed to this diameter. However, unless the missing jambs were restored also, such an arch would have an inherent flaw because the reduced arch would have insufficient support beneath. Since in 1989 the gate was very much still in use by vehicles, it was impractical to restore the arch jambs and consequently reduce road width by 11in. One could argue also that it would be wrong to restore a feature which has been absent for more than a century. Hence, with no restored jambs, the restored arch had to be built to a size slightly larger than would otherwise be correct.[145]

As the road arch was built, first the four springers were reinstated in their original positions, then the rest was constructed of new stone. In order to reinforce the arch's strength, plans for the rebuilding incorporated between each stone a concealed steel shear key set in strong mortar, intended to limit any movement between adjacent voussoirs. Also, the plans included a ⅜ in. stainless steel tang projecting upward from each stone and set in epoxy resin to strengthen the arch-to-wall bond. On the inner side of the new arch keystone was inscribed the date 1989. This date, placed inconspicuously, will prevent confusion of this restored arch with original features.[146]

As with the large stones inserted in the façade, some criticism was heard of alignment in the new arch. Particularly on the upstream side, the new stones appear to align poorly with the old stones. Again, though, this is partly due to wear and mutilation of some of the old arch stones. If the old stones retained their original faces, then the arch soffit would be more smooth. Instead the new arch stones were placed close to the position where the old faces would line up if they remained intact (Figs. 51 and 52).[147]

When the 1989 conservation works were planned, consideration was given to protection of the gate once the works had been finished. It was difficult to enforce the three ton vehicle weight limit and the 10 ft. 3 in. height limit at all times. Clearly, this could be done only if an officer were to be on duty at the bridge or some sophisticated meter system were in place permanently. Since no permanent closure to vehicles was anticipated until some undefined later date, it might be wise to install some type of protection for the interim period. Measures considered included metal 'goal posts', a flashing light warning system, and the installation of kerbs to guide vehicles through the centre of the archway. Although a potential eyesore, the goal posts may have been the most simple and effective solution. Such a firm physical barrier would exclude vehicles that are too high. Admittedly, steel beams would be unattractive. However, they would protect the gate, and they could be removed as soon as permanent pedestrianization occurred. But, neither the goal posts nor any other protective equipment was installed during or following the works. Not surprisingly, gouges caused by high vehicles were to be seen at the south-west arch soffit only weeks after the works had been unveiled. This unsolved problem was illustrated vividly in the *Monmouthshire Beacon* in April 1990 and October 1991. Each has a photograph showing a lorry, clearly higher than the limit, inching through the new south-west archway. In June 1990 came a rare prosecution following an event at the bridge. A man from Bristol was fined after driving a lorry under the gate which had damaged the arch masonry and exceeded the weight limit by more than double. Thus, by six months after the 1989 works, insufficient protection had allowed gouges and chips to occur to the new archway, although no cracking in the arch or wall had yet occurred. A similar incident on 23 October 1991 likewise resulted in a fine for a Cheltenham lorry driver. The scars and damage might add to the feeling of antiquity, but such assaults must undermine structural stability.[148]

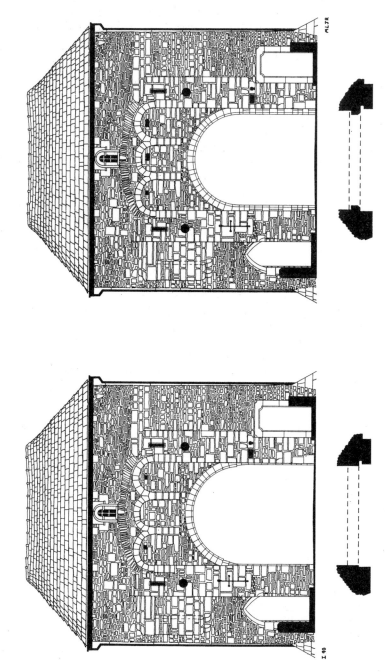

Fig. 52. Drawings of the Monnow Gate south-west elevation and plans of the south-west road arch at road level after the conservation work of October/November 1989, and the gate as it might appear after restoration of the jambs and archway.

A more serious incident occurred when the south-western arch was struck by a vehicle on 18 December 1992. Two of the voussoirs had slight damage, but two others had their lower halves shorn off. As the damage was severe, but the arch had not become unsafe, scheduled monument consent was required prior to replacing the stones with spares from the 1989 works.

Future Development

The obvious prime future desire at Monnow Bridge will be closure of the bridge to all motorized vehicles. This single action would lead to a marked change in the monument's deterioration. Also, it would allow easy appreciation and examination of the building and possible exploitation of it as a tourist attraction.

Regular staffed opening of the gate would be welcome, allowing visitors to inspect the interior and to see the medieval defensive remains. Since the north-east wall of the tower room is largely flat and featureless, a couple of permanent display panels/cases could be installed giving an interpretation of the monument's past. Electrical lighting could be installed, providing that this is well planned and *discreet*. Better than putting displays in the tower would be a separate interpretation centre in nearby premises. A small display room could accompany a shop and ticket desk.

Once the bridge has been pedestrianized, measures could be taken to correct the recent changes to the south-west road arch's design. Resetting of the arch could occur so that its size and shape returns to that which existed before recent works and before the jambs under the arch were removed. To ensure that the arch then created would be safe, the jambs could be restored (Fig. 52) and/or a concealed steel beam could be inserted at room floor level, above the road arch, thus relieving the arch of its considerable burden and spreading this weight to the side walls. It would be a matter for debate whether or not jambs lost over a century ago should be restored. However, an inserted beam would allow the arch to be reset correctly and safely without rebuilding the lost jambs.

It is likely that closure of the bridge and the opening of a new one downstream would lead to removal of the St Thomas's Square roundabout. It is suggested that at the same time the road leading up to the bridge could be reduced to its original width. The road would no longer carry vehicles, and the adjacent garden could be expanded to cover the entire area of the terrace of houses demolished in the 1920s. The stone cross on the roundabout could be dismantled and re-erected as a focal point to the enlarged garden. A more radical development would be to return the existing garden to its residential use. A terrace of houses stood here for centuries, and it would not be difficult to erect cottages or flats to a design in keeping with the historic site.

Ideally, once the bridge and roadway are closed to traffic, the owners might be in a position to enter into an agreement with Cadw: Welsh Historic Monuments wherein the latter body could take over responsibility for care of the monument. Monnow Bridge and Gate could benefit from Cadw's experience in maintaining, interpreting, and opening ancient monuments to the public.

Description

Monnow Bridge and Gate can be described conveniently in the relative order in which they were constructed. Thus, this account will begin down at the river and progress up to the tower and its interior (Fig. 53). A flight of steps between the bridge and the cattle market leads down to the river.

River Bed
The river at Monnow Bridge flows over sand, gravel, and loose rocks which rest on a bed of reddish-brown silty clay mudstone (known as marl). From this point downstream the river is fairly straight. But, above the bridge the Monnow curves to the right around the town. Much of the river's volume flows through the two south-western bridge spans, creating a variety of depths of gravel and marl across the river. The Monmouth flood scheme investigations allowed a profile of the river bed. The marl bedrock is found between 50 mm. and 2,700 mm. below the common water level, bare or overlain by gravel or silt. However, the normal water level increased by around 670 mm. after the construction of a weir of boulders some metres below the bridge in October 1992.

Differential flow volumes also lead to deposition at the town side of the bridge. Here, above the tower pier is an area of sand and coarse gravel deposition, and, at the north-eastern span, silt builds up with each temporary increase of river level. The trial pits of 1983 revealed a 3,000 mm. depth of gravel and silt near the tower pier compared to 400 mm. near pier two. Similar differences were found between borehole samples in 1984. Figure 54 is a plan and elevation of the bridge and river bed.[149]

MONNOW BRIDGE
Construction Materials
Monnow Bridge is built of about seven types of stone. Two of these stone types form the bulk of building material used, and all of them were probably quarried within ten miles of Monmouth. The stone types can be described as follows:[150] (1) an old red sandstone; (2) a buff-coloured coarse sandstone with occasional pebbles of vein quartz; (3) a micaceous siltstone, greenish grey, with fine

Fig. 53. Monnow Bridge viewed from the south in the late 1920s, before building of the cattle market steps.

laminated bedding, possibly carboniferous; (4) a grey carboniferous limestone, with some fossils; (5) a grey old red sandstone, with no pebbles and no noticeable lamination; (6) a buff-coloured conglomerate, having a coarse sand matrix with bands of fine vein quartz pebbles and a few random larger pebbles; and (7) a sandstone with limonite (ochre), being a variety of type 2. Additionally, some Hollington red sandstone from Staffordshire was introduced during the 1989 conservation scheme. Stone types 1 and 2 are most prevalent.

The mortar used is of fine gravel and lime, with a few areas of a sea sand mortar with visible minute sea fauna.

Piers

In the days when Monnow Bridge was first built in stone it would have been inconceivable to consider attempting a single arched span of the river. Thus, at least one pier resting in the river was required, and in this instance two were used. The bridge piers had to rest on a firm foundation to ensure that there would be no subsidence and to prevent undercutting by the river. Shuttering would be needed around the site of the proposed pier so that excavation could proceed easily. Ideally, the stone pier would be built directly upon the natural rock bed underlying any sand or gravel. If a reasonably deep excavation failed to reveal a solid bed, then the

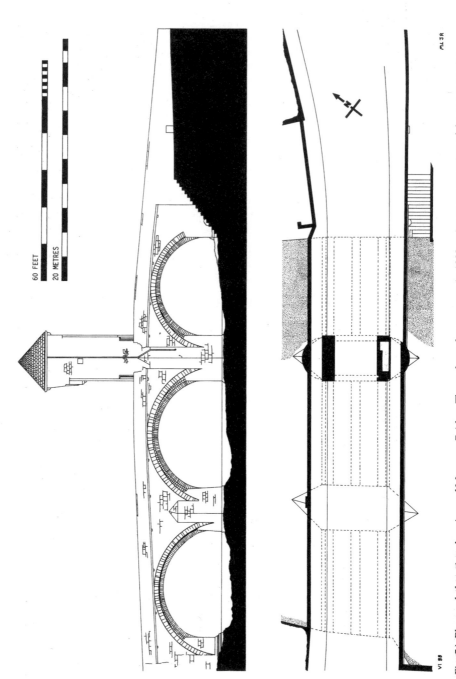

60 FEET

20 METRES

Fig. 54. Plan and elevation drawings of Monnow Bridge. These show the structure in 1988, prior to construction of the concrete pier protection apron and before alteration of the cattle market steps.

pier foundations could be constructed using some combination of a coffer dam, piles, or a raft. Under the coffer dam method timber stakes and shuttering would be driven into the river bed to form a fairly watertight perimeter to the foundations. Then the interior would be filled with rubble and cement up to the top of the shuttering. On this firm base the pier would rise. For greater stability piles could be driven into the bed, perhaps combined with a submerged raft of timbers.

Examination of the Monnow Bridge piers has shown that, despite the relatively shallow depth of the marl bedrock here, the piers were not built upon a solid substrate. Cores were taken from four boreholes into the piers, and excavations adjacent to the piers were undertaken in preparation for the Monmouth flood alleviation works at Monnow Bridge of 1988/90.[151] The boreholes indicated gravel under the piers, suggesting that the medieval bridge builders did not excavate so that the entire pier could be built upon rock. Later, during the 1988 excavation, on top of gravel overlying the marl, was found the substantial horizontal oak sole plate 0.35 m. in depth running along the north-west/south-east axis of the tower pier (Fig. 50). Jointed into the top of this is a vertical timber extending 0.85 m. up to the under-side of the pier facework. Behind these timbers in the pier foundations the coarse rubble and cement core was visible without any masonry facework.

Ordinarily, looking at the bottom of the tower pier wall facework, one can see the stonework splayed outward twice, the larger offset directly above the smaller. Taking the joint above the upper splay as a reference point, the table [152] below summarizes the relative vertical positions of the foundation features.

Pier Foundation Features

Relative depths of the features under the eastern side of the downstream cutwater of the tower pier, listed relative to the joint directly above the upper splayed course at the bottom of the pier, and relative to ordnance datum. Also listed relative to OD are features encountered down the R1 borehole. All measurements are in metres.

Feature	Relative to the joint	Relative to OD	Along R1 above OD
OD bench mark on Monnow Gate	7.675	20.55	
Joint over the upper splayed course	0.000	12.875	
Bottom of pier facework	– 0.478	12.397	
Top of vertical timber	– 0.528	12.347	
Top of sole plate	– 1.378	11.497	11.50
Bottom of sole plate	– 1.728	11.147	
Gravel under horizontal timber	– 1.925		10.95
Upper surface of marl	– 2.975		9.90
Ordnance datum	–12.875	0.000	

The offsets or splays visible on the tower pier originally existed at the lower edge of the two abutments and all sides of both piers. From these offsets the piers were built upward with courses of fine ashlar work on the outer face, mostly built of old red sandstone and micaceous siltstone, whilst the core was progressively filled in with rubble and cement. After only a couple of courses of walling, building of the bridge spans began with erection of the arch rings, that is, the three projecting bands of stonework under the spans. Much of this ashlar on the piers is smooth-faced. The stone with a tooled face around much of pier two is due to the replacement of damaged facework during the bridge repairs of 1892. Much of it appears to have come from a quarry at the Buckholt, just north of Monmouth. Also in 1892, the double splays originally around the pier two bottom were replaced with a series of small squared offsets extending down far below the nominal bed level (Fig. 49). Until the flood scheme works, the remains of parts of the wooden shuttering used in 1892 were visible embedded in concrete at the cutwaters of pier two (Fig. 55).

Cutwaters

The piers are six-sided with sharply pointed cutwaters to divide the river flow. Pointed cutwaters allow less pressure on the bridge than those that are rounded or flat. Both piers and their cutwaters are asymmetrical, with the tower pier orientated perpendicularly to the bridge axis and pier two placed obliquely to point upstream. Along with building of the three bridge spans, pier building progressed upward until just above the extrados (upper, outer face) of the span arches. With the whole river thus spanned, a rubble layer would have been spread over the length of the bridge surface, and the ashlar side walls would have been carried up to form parapets. Over both piers the cutwaters were

Fig. 55. The remains of a shoring timber embedded in the concrete pier protection at the eastern side of pier two, September 1987.

carried up to form triangular refuges continuous with the parapet walls (Fig. 18). Considering the five metre width of the original bridge, it is clear why these projections were called refuges.

Three Bridge Spans

The arch rings projecting under the main spans at Monnow Bridge are an example of an innovation in bridge building used commonly by medieval builders (Figs. 56 and 62). Bridge arch rings are comparable to the ribs used in medieval church vaulting. Like these ribs the arch rings were employed to improve strength and economy whilst erecting broad arches. A wooden centring or falsework was required over the top of which the stone arch could be built course by course (Fig. 33). The economy afforded by an arch ring or a vault rib was seen in the amount of falsework necessary and in the number of good-quality dressed arch stones required. Rather than needing centring as wide as the bridge and the use of entirely dressed stones under the spans, arch rings allowed discrete bands of voussoirs each only requiring its own narrow falsework. The space between these individual centrings could be bridged by planks or boards upon which could be built a webbing of flagstones, ashlar

Fig. 56. The south-western span of Monnow Bridge looking south in November 1985. Three projecting arch rings can be seen. Also, right of the nearest arch ring is the original chamfered edge of the bridge span. The section beyond that is one of the six Victorian extensions of the bridge.

stonework, rubble, or, as at Monnow Bridge, elongated and irregularly coursed stonework. The boards and centring would have been 'struck' out once the builders were sure that the masonry could support itself, sometimes in the Middle Ages as much as several months or more after the construction.[153]

It has been suggested that the infill between arch rings transfers the weight of the span and traffic above to the rings or ribs, which in turn transfer the mass to the bridge piers. However, except perhaps when the infill is of flags, this is clearly not true. Particularly in bridge spans, where the space above the span arch is filled with rubble and cement, the span is thought of as a cohesive structure standing due to its massive solidity. The main structural advantage of the arch rings is not to hold up the span, but their character as a true arch preserves the span's arch contour and prevents deformation of the span that could occur with a facing of flags or rubble alone.[154]

There is some mixing of stone, but the outer arch ring spans contain mostly the buff-coloured coarse sandstone with old red sandstone more noticeable at the middle.

As well as at the arch rings, true arches were also constructed at the edges of the bridge spans to form the bottom of the upstream and downstream faces of the bridge. Although Monnow Bridge was widened in Victorian times, these stones are still visible under the bridge. In all but one of these edges the stones are chamfered at the corner. Here the arch ring stones are thin with the slightest of convergence towards the interior edge of the arch (the intrados). The Victorian voussoirs at the edge of the spans, on the other hand, are bold and more noticeably wedge-shaped.

Bridge Widening Spans
The refuges at Monnow Bridge have been removed. This was done due to building of the tower, some thirty years after erection of the bridge, and due to widening of the bridge to allow for footpaths. Under the spans one can see a gap beyond the original chamfered bridge edge where new widening spans were added which were bonded into the pier cutwaters. These widening spans were built on each side of the three original spans, each being slightly different in width and height evidently in order to adjust the carriageway orientation and camber. Although these spans were added some six hundred years after the original work, the stone make-up is quite similar. The infill is composed mostly of old red sandstone with a little laminated micaceous siltstone. The voussoir stones now at the bridge edges are of similar material to the arch rings, with the addition of some of the type seven sandstone with limonite.

Parapet Walls
When the present upstream and downstream sides of the bridge were built, undoubtedly much of the original stonework was reused from the unwidened

bridge, mostly of the prevalent old red sandstone. The parapet walls atop these sides likewise show some mixture of materials. The fact that the upstream and downstream parapets were built several years apart is also reflected in their design.

The downstream parapet wall resembles most closely its ancient predecessor. Both parapets are normal double-skinned walls of ashlar of varying quality, with occasional through-stones, and topped with coping. Downstream a physical division exists between the bridge side and the parapet wall. Crossing the bridge just above the extrados of the bridge widening arches is a course of flat through-stones which slightly projects beyond the wall below and is supported by (originally twelve) decorative corbels (Figs. 42 and 53). This course, level with the bridge roadway, serves as a foundation for the downstream parapet, built of the same materials as the bridge sides. Opposite the Barley Mow public house some of the mortar with sea sand can be seen. But, elsewhere, the sand and lime mortar prevails. Large old red sandstone and grey old red sandstone coping stones cap the wall, many of which survive from before the nineteenth century. These are the ones that show signs of cramping. Until the bridge was widened the coping stones had small depressions near their ends. Metal staples anchored in lead were attached in these holes across the joints of adjacent stones. Near the tower, and east of it, several of these formerly cramped stones can be seen. The coping without evidence of cramping dates from after this downstream side was widened.

Although it was rebuilt earlier than the other, the upstream parapet was constructed to a different design from that which had existed before and some new materials were used (Fig. 57). No through-stone foundation was used here; the parapet is only divided from the bridge side by being projected slightly over it. The sandstone masonry is capped by an uncramped coping of long old red sandstone blocks with top side edges chamfered. The height of the wall and the new coping blocks are what most noticeably changed when this side was widened and the wall was rebuilt in the 1820s. Above pier two the parapet is slightly thickened and the coping contains a circular metal scar. Here for seventy or so years, from the early 1890s, stood a street lamp.

Footpaths

The present footpaths rest to the sides of the original bridge and approximately over the Victorian bridge widenings. The original parapet walls stood about where the path kerbstones are now. The pavement surfaces of geometric bricks are a recent, and arguably unfortunate, replacement of concrete flagstones, which themselves replaced stone flags. Utility pipelines must occasionally cross rivers, and the bridge serves to carry these as well as vehicles and pedestrians. Pipes exist under both paths for the gas, water, electricity, and telephone authorities. Since bricks are thicker than flagstones, the presence of pipes directly under the paths brought an increase in path height when the bricks were laid.[155]

Fig. 57. Monnow Bridge viewed from
the north in December 1985.

Of the stones making up the bridge spans, the voussoirs have more depth
than the rubble infill. Thus, along the extrados the voussoirs project upwards
slightly beyond the rubble surface. Gravel and loose rubble fills in between the
arch stone tops. Fine sandstone gravel forms a level surface under the bricks. A
welcome change when the brick paths were created was the reinstatement of
stone kerbs. For some time beforehand concrete kerbstones had prevailed. Metal
kerbing had been employed on the Monmouth side of the gate, some of which
survives opposite the public house.

MONNOW GATE EXTERIOR

The medieval tower resting on pier one is a mutilated remnant of a building
type once seen frequently in Britain, the defensive bridge gate. In the eighteenth
century their defensive roles had long since ceased, and, being long before the
now popular concept of conservation, increasingly their nuisance as a bottleneck
to already narrow bridges was considered sufficient reason for demolition.
Substantial town gates on bridges existed at Shrewsbury, Chester, Durham,
York, Bedford, and at several other towns lying adjacent to rivers. Several
impressive bridge gates still survive across Europe (Fig. 58)[156], but only two
remain in Britain. The other British medieval fortified bridge is at Warkworth,
Northumberland (Fig. 59). This fine bridge over the River Coquet retains

Fig. 58. Sketches of European fortified bridges standing and demolished. From the top left, clockwise, they are the Mardol Gate on the Old Welsh Bridge at Shrewsbury; Dee Bridge, Chester; *Pont Valentré* at Cahors, France; Froome Bridge, Bristol; Old London Bridge; and the *Pont Vieux* at Orthez, France.

parapet refuges over a massive central pier. The tower, now ruinous, and bridge are of the late fourteenth century. The primary type difference that sets Monnow Bridge apart from Warkworth Bridge is that Warkworth's defensive structure is a *tête-du-pont*, lying on land at the head of the bridge on the town side rather than actually standing upon the bridge.

Fig. 59. Drawing of Warkworth Bridge after an etching dated 1834 by T.M. Richardson (1784–1848). The gate is just over the bridge. Beyond is the keep of Warkworth Castle.

The Monnow Gate that we see today bears evidence of many of the innovations in defensive architecture of the Middle Ages all concentrated in one small building. Here there are or were a portcullis, machicolations, plain arrow loops, cross-shaped arrow slits with oillets, massive wooden doors, and a battlemented parapet (Figs. 60–3). The room above housed the portcullis winching mechanism, although later it served as a lock-up and as a dwelling. We must remember that originally the bridge was barely wider than the main road arch. The piers were as now, pier two being topped by large refuges and pier one supporting the gatehouse. The asymmetrical pedestrian passageways were not necessary when the tower was erected. After noting these two recent arches we shall continue with the more mature features.

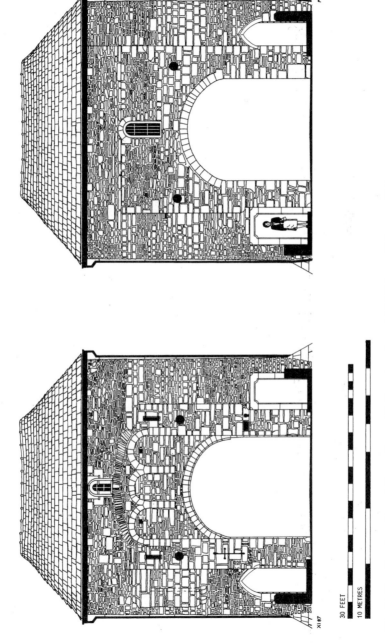

Fig. 60. Elevation drawings of the south-west (left) and north-east (right) faces of Monnow Gate.

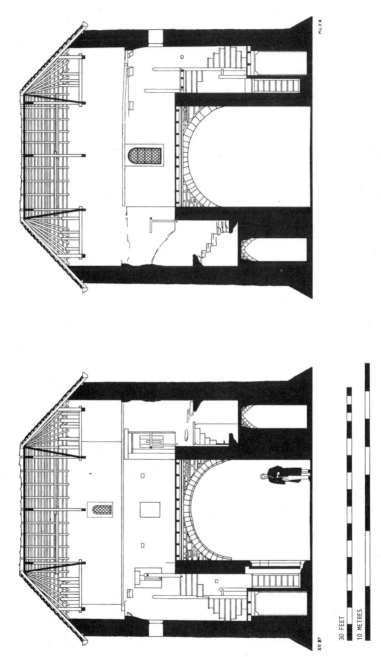

Fig. 61. Sectional drawings through the tower centre looking south-west (left) and north-east (right).

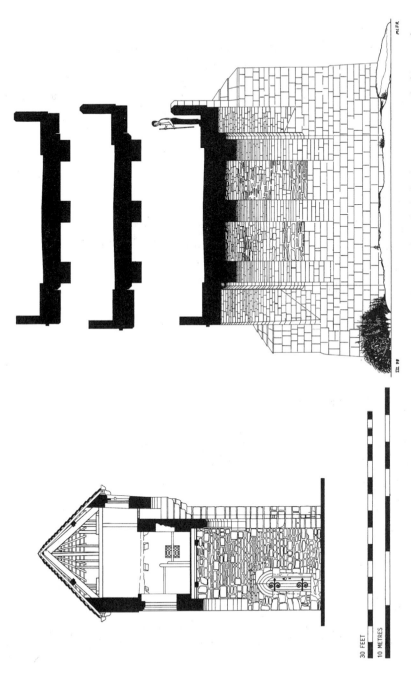

30 FEET

10 METRES

Fig. 62. A sectional drawing through the tower centre looking south-east, and sections through the bridge span centres looking south-west (top, Overmonnow span; centre, Monmouth span; bottom, middle span and pier two).

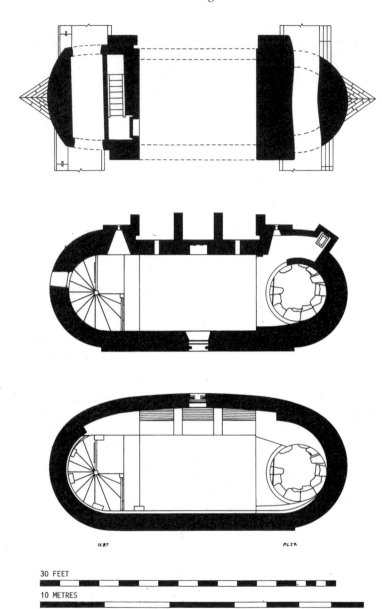

Fig. 63. Plan drawings of the tower at road level (top), at room level (centre), and at the wall-walk.

Gothic Passageway

First to be added of the pedestrian ways was the pointed, gothic style passage (Fig. 64). Within the tower at this point existed the original stone newel (or circular) stair to the tower room. Thus, when this passageway was created the original tower entrance and stairway were destroyed and repositioned at the opposite side of the road arch passage. It must be recalled that the site of the pedestrian arch was outwith the bridge width so that, beyond the expense of new arches and labour, platforms were required each side from the bridge to the passage.

Although very few dressed stones were used to complete the lancet arches at each end of the tunnel, two different stone types were employed, old red sandstone and grey old red sandstone, both bevelled on the inner edge. The passage itself is serpentine to allow for a slight thickening of the outer tower wall. The passage is ceiled by red sandstone flags.

Walling Materials

Just above the gothic arch on the western side are many small rectangular blocks of old red sandstone. This particular type of block, not precisely squared and usually without a perfectly flat face, can be seen dotted all over the gate. These are mostly the result of repairs to the facework executed in the 1890s. For decades before that time it appears that little maintenance had occurred at the

Fig. 64. Monnow Gate's gothic style pedestrian passage viewed from the north-east. The photograph was taken on 26 October 1985, before footpath resurfacing.

tower except for that necessary due to safety. For example, engravings and photographs show that when the pointed arch was inserted the masons did not make good the surrounding stonework. Thus, this part of the tower stood in decay until the 1890's cosmetic work. In this project all decayed or damaged facework was removed and/or filled with old red sandstone blocks.

Elsewhere on the gate are large ashlar blocks surviving intact from the original building. The quoins of the two projecting walls each side of the main road arch contain such substantial well-dressed, close-jointed pieces of red and grey old red sandstone with the occasional few of buff-coloured coarse sandstone. Two-thirds of the way up the tower walls, around the curved sides over the river, there are large stretches of this ashlar, unbroken by damage and repairs.

If one stands very close to the tower and looks up the walls, particularly on the north-eastern side, one sees numerous tiny wooden stubs sticking out. These are nothing more than the anchors which held a myriad of Victorian advertising and voting placards. Correspondence in the *Beacon* indicates that placarding the gate tower was seen as scurrilous by such concerned citizens as the person with the *nom de plume* Antiquitatis Amator in 1881, but for advertisers the prominent position was irresistible.

Rectangular Passage

Some twenty years after the gothic passage was built the opposite side of the tower was pierced for another (Fig. 65). It is difficult now to imagine that in the 1840s there was sufficient traffic to make a second pedestrian arch a necessity. Nevertheless, the rectangular passage was made, yet again demanding the destruction of the tower stairway. Since now the tower abutment south-east of the road had to accommodate a stair and a passage, the design of the gothic walkway could not be duplicated. Also, the lack of space dictated the materials to be employed. Between the new staircase and the passageway was placed a brick partition supporting a wooden passage ceiling. At each end of the passage the lintels and jambs are carved from a buff-coloured conglomerate stone, otherwise unusual on this building. The jambs are rebated and the lintels have some decoration; the inner corners projecting inwards as quarter circles, reflected as incised marks at the outer corners. The lintels are slightly curved to follow the tower wall. It is unfortunate that flat lintels were applied without provision of relieving arches above. The south-western lintel succumbed to the strain by cracking many years ago. Obliquely placed steel bolts were inserted in March 1988 to prevent the centre of the lintel from falling.

Main Gate Passage

The road passageway, although still at its original width, has experienced much change. Considering the period in which the gatehouse was erected, the main arches are likely to have been originally in the gothic, pointed style. The arch voussoirs did not die into the passage side walls, as they do now. Instead blocks continued from the arch down the walls to form jambs. Although the arch itself

Fig. 65. The rectangular passageway viewed from the south-west (26 October 1985) after replacement of the footpath flagstones by geometric bricks.

was changed, the jambs survived until quite recently. The projection of the lowest surviving arch voussoirs indicates where the stones below have been removed.

The present south-western facing arch is entirely new, all of the voussoirs being replaced firstly in 1982, after damage to the tower caused by the double-decker bus, then again in 1989. The lower voussoirs, those that die into the side walls, are of much greater antiquity. They are massive and solid, much like those of the now elder north-eastern archway. The new stones, slightly smaller than the old stones at the sides, are nevertheless an improvement over the 1982 arch stones. Copying the previous arch and the ancient stones, the lower front edge of the arch is chamfered, and the lower back edge is rebated to receive the now long-lost doors. One of the hinge pivots on which these doors hung remains high up on the north-western side wall.

Directly in front of the main south-western arch on each side can be seen the grooves which held the portcullis gate. Ordinarily this gate would have been held up in the raised position with enough clearance underneath for a mounted rider to pass easily. But, when defence was required, the archway doors would be barred and the gate could be released. Its wide bars and tremendous weight would halt attackers, whilst archers and crossbowmen within the tower could spray fire from the arrow slits and the roof walkway.

Unlike the south-western arch, the north-eastern does not appear to have been mutilated or to have received any significant rebuilding. The arch meets the side walls smoothly and is composed primarily of voussoirs of old red sandstone and the buff-coloured coarse sandstone. With no chamfer or rebate, the front and back edges are rounded.

Within the gate passage items of note are the present and former tower entrances and the passage ceiling. The joists of the tower room are supported by two visible oak beams. These beams, built into and right through the side walls, date from repairs of the early 1800s. Between the beams a boarded ceiling has been applied hung by battens attached to the beam sides. Just below the boarding on the south-eastern side an oblong hole remains which once served to ventilate the space when the beams were hidden by a ceiling attached to their under-sides, a Victorian development recently reversed.

The present tower doorway is of a convincingly thirteenth-century design (Fig. 66). Above the door two carved stones form a two-centred arch with a chamfered inner edge and rebated back. Below this, on the opposite side to the hinges, a door jamb of oak is employed to engage the door bolt. The door itself is of elm boards with floral strapwork hinges, an escutcheon around the keyhole, a round spirally fluted handle, and a floral escutcheon under the handle. However, despite its appearance, the entire arrangement is of nineteenth-century date. On the opposite wall directly across from the present door one can see clearly the position of the first doorway, of comparable size and evidently

Fig. 66. Doorway to the tower stairway, 28 September 1988.

flat-topped. When the door position was switched, all new materials were employed rather than simply transferring the old components.

Just beyond the scar of the old doorway at the eastern corner there is a mark incised into the stone in the form of a line with an arrow underneath. This is an Ordnance Survey bench mark. Apparently carved into the stone *circa* 1880, the centre of the line, at the top of the arrow, is at OS coordinates SO 5046 1251 and was measured at 20.55 metres above sea-level at Newlyn, Cornwall, in 1967.

Arrow Slits and the Garderobe

Opening off what was the original stairway on the front of the building is a cross-shaped arrow slit. Since the gap of the slit is only 44 mm. wide, there was little chance of harm from attackers outside. The slit is cross-shaped with oillets at the end of each arm. At a comparable place on the opposite side of the main road arch is a much worn oillet next to the brass plaque. It is likely that this is an oillet from a cross arrow loop once existing symmetrically opposite the intact one.

Higher up the front walls two plain rectangular arrow slits open off embrasures of the tower room. The one above the cross slit is situated in the passage to the garderobe. The garderobe is the large projection on corbels situated above the gothic passage. This type of medieval toilet is a common feature of castle architecture. Ordinarily such privies were atop a shaft that emptied into a moat or a pit. Here, though, the gate porter's waste could discharge directly into the river. Provision of such a garderobe for the tower room points out that originally the gate must have been occupied continually or at least frequently.

Each side of the main road arch, just below the plain arrow loops, are two round metal plates. These plates are on the ends of the tie rods running through the tower at just below the tower room floor level. The rods run through obliquely so that the empty space of the stairwells is employed. Plates at the other end are found on the north-eastern side of the building. The rods and plates were added in *c.*1890 literally to arrest the apparently growing separation of the front and back of the tower.

Windows

In the age when this building was used for defence, it would have been unwise to place any large windows on the front, south-western face. Here only the safe loops could provide light and ventilation. However, on the town side or over the water there was ample opportunity for windows, although these were unlikely to be glazed before the mid-fifteenth century. The existing window arrangements are mostly the result of Victorian work. The main tower window now is that facing Monnow Street. There is another over the wooden staircase facing towards the cattle market. Both windows are glazed with diamond paned leaded lights, a type of glazing that came into common use around 1500. The south-eastern window, facing the market, is square and placed in a rough embrasure splayed outward. A simple wooden moulding holds the leaded window. The main window (Fig. 67) is a much grander affair secured outside by

Fig. 67. The main, north-eastern, tower
room window, 5 June 1988.

three vertical and two flat horizontal bars and surrounded by a round-headed
roll moulding running down to the sill. This north-eastern window also is not
original. A smaller square leaded window existed here before this one was
inserted in 1832. The moulded surround is of more than one date. The upper
portion that has a dark yellow colour is the original work, apparently not of
carved stone but of cement and sand. The work is exactly contemporary with
the massive corbels under the roof eaves. The rest of the surround is completed
in a sandstone concrete. This work, which is inferior to the work above, appears
to be a repair of the 1940s when during the Second World War several lorries
assaulted the gateway. Likewise the prominent arch stones over the window
were changed at that time. Formerly, the projecting line of masonry running
across the gate over the window crossed through the arch stones.

On the front (south-west) of the building is a small attic window under the
eaves (Fig. 68). It now closely resembles a sixteenth-century garderobe passage
window at Howick house, near Chepstow. However, the window at Monnow
Gate did not exist before the eighteenth century and appears to date from
shortly after 1705, when the gate was converted to a dwelling of two floors. Like
the surround of the main north-eastern window, this one also has suffered from
inept repairs. The window has leaded lights set in a wooden board which did
not appear before the late 1890s. Before that time there was no glazing. The

Fig. 68. The south-western attic window, 5 June 1988.

surround is secured by a vertical diamond-shaped bar which has two flat horizontals. According to old drawings and photographs, originally the surround was an elegantly carved affair, round headed with a roll moulding in two orders (i.e. two concentric steps) down to the sill. These were crossed just below the arch by raised horizontal blocks resembling abaci which projected into the opening slightly. By some time in the 1890s the mouldings must have become severely decayed since shortly before 1897 the lower portion was rendered over rudely with mortar, obscuring the original shape. One assumes that the decayed two-ordered moulding still remains under the modern mortar.

Machicolation and the Parapet

Below the south-western attic window a curve of many thin sandstone blocks bedded vertically forms a relieving arch in order to transfer some of the great weight above off the main road arch and the three arches of machicolation (Fig. 69). Above these machicolation arches once stood the battlemented parapet behind which there was a walkway at the top of the wall. The parapet bowed outward, as the wall here does still, and the projecting portion is carried on the three arches which rest on two sets of four corbels set in the wall over the road arch and end on corbels set into the side walls. The arch voussoirs are of a fine sandstone, with a buff colour and some cross lamination. Upwardly the corbels

Fig. 69. Three machicolation arches and the relieving arch above the main road arch at Monnow Gate, 5 June 1988.

are stepped outward so that the wall above projects beyond the wall below. The wall-walk at roof level, also called an alure, was carried straight across above the road arch, the bowed out parapet being used to provide shafts between the corbels through which could be thrown missiles upon the enemy and water to douse any fire set at the gate.

Around the sides of the tower, bands of ashlar stone are present up to just beyond the machicolation. Amidst the highest surviving course on the south side was the wall-walk drain, lost in the 1950s. At the north-eastern side a horizontal step in the masonry a little above the window likewise indicates the position of the former parapet bottom. All around the tower at this point the stonework (old red and grey old red sandstone) is clearly of a different quality to that above. When the building was converted to a dwelling the parapet here was rebuilt as a solid wall and the roof, formerly concealed, was placed upon the new walling. At Manorbier, Usk, and Kidwelly Castles, and some other fortified buildings of comparable date, crenelated parapets were raised or converted to solid walls simply by filling in the open spaces of the parapet (the crenels). Here at Monnow Gate there is now no evidence of this practice. However, in engravings and several photographs dating from before the 1880s (e.g. Fig. 29) several large vertical joints in the walling under the eaves suggest that a similar procedure may have been followed.

There are just a few stones at parapet level which appear to have the remains of a limewash. It is not clear whether or not these are blocks in their original position or are insertions. But, it is very likely that for much of its existence Monnow Gate was whitewashed. In the thirteenth century it was just as common a practice to whiten the exterior of such defensive buildings as castles as it was for modest cottages.

Roof

Atop the rebuilt parapet is the roof that was remodelled in the early eighteenth century. This is 'supported' by four great corbels on each side of the gate. These corbels do not really hold up anything. The only weight that they carry are the ends of a few rafters and part of the wall-plate.

Reflecting the shape of the walling below, the roof is asymmetrical. The straight back edge continues as semicircles around the sides. But, due to the machicolation and former wall-walk, the front edge curves outward. The roof itself is composed of seventeen courses of tilestones which decrease in size from eaves to ridge. Clay tiles protect the ridge. Under the eaves, where the rafters cross the wall top, they rest on horizontal wall-plate timbers. Behind the wall-plate the gaps between the rafters are filled with brick and roughly laid stonework.

MONNOW GATE INTERIOR

Entering through the tower door, one steps into a dark stairway and up to a gloomy room above. Since the first flight of steps is housed within a wall, space is very limited. This flight is bound by the space between the roadway wall and the rectangular passageway's brick partition. For the first stairway, there is an open flight of seven steps up to a small landing resting on timbers let into the stone and brick walls. One step upward to the left brings one on to the passageway ceiling lit by a piece of heavy glass. The steps of the following circular staircase up to the tower room are supported on beams let into the curved tower end wall and, at the other end, by a wooden newel post over the brick partition (Fig. 70). Twelve steps with risers run upwards counterclockwise, the thirteenth step being another landing bound by a rail from the newel post top. There are several holes in the curved side wall. These once supported the beams holding up a former stairway. From the top landing, a further step to the right leads on to the top of a road passage side wall and to the floor level of the room proper.

Tower Room

The tower room (Figs. 71 and 37) apparently has never been supplied with electricity or gas for lighting or heating, and it takes some minutes before one's eyes adjust to see any details of the interior. In winter-time the interior can be exceedingly dark and cold. A chimney once projected out of the roof. Thus, although the interior is now cold and barren, one can imagine the inside being warm and fairly well lit when there was a fireplace and the current room was subdivided with partitions and a low ceiling. The rooms would have been much

Fig. 70. The wooden staircases viewed from the upper landing, 28 September 1988.

Fig. 71. The tower room looking north-north-west from the alure ledge, 28 September 1988. The machicolation chutes and attic window are to the left.

lighter due to whitewash on the walls, traces of which remain.

Around much of the tower wall near the stairway a break in the masonry forms an offset at a little above one's head. Along this ledge holes exist in the wall and five corbels remain just below it. These features mark the point at which the timber of the original roof rested, and it is also the point where later the new attic floor rested when the tower was converted to a dwelling. At first the room was very low with a roof of shallow pitch positioned at this ledge. The walling above was the battlemented parapet exterior to the room, and the large ledge at the front side was the wall-walk, also exterior to the room. Four hundred years later, conversion to a dwelling for the gatekeeper caused a transformation. The parapet was rebuilt as solid walling with a new roof atop similar to but much larger than the former one. This roof had a dormer window at the rear to light the attic room created when a new floor was inserted where the old roof had been. Now that the inserted floor has been removed, the tower room is spacious although still dark. In former days, when there were low ceilings and the floors were divided into separate rooms, the tower interior must have been claustrophobic by today's standards. We must remember though that in those centuries the common man was accustomed to compact hovels and when first built this was not a dwelling but a workplace. Also, then the average man was a little shorter in stature.

At the topmost stairway landing is one of the two plain arrow loops on the south-western front. The wall is quite deep here, and the embrasure is splayed so that the archer could observe attackers whilst positioned away from the opening with relative safety. A similar loop is positioned at the other end in the passage to the garderobe. The wall being much thinner there, the embrasure is very shallow. Both loops were not glazed until just before the turn of this century. Then plain panes surrounded by wooden boards were inserted, presumably to exclude the elements.[157]

Windows

As mentioned earlier there are three main windows in the tower room (Fig. 72). Each has diamond-shaped panes surrounded by lead cames. There is a border of rectangular panes of lengths comparable to the diamond dimensions. The window over the stairway is roughly square, unopenable, and set in a wooden moulding. The other two windows are round-headed to match the wall openings. The attic light also is unopenable and is set in a wooden board. Hinges connect the large north-eastern window to its metal frame. A handled latch secures the window by a slot in the frame. As the window is large and prone to buckling, there are three horizontal bars to which the leading is wired. The window has a slant-sided embrasure bound above by the former roof/floor ledge.

Tower Room Furnishings

At the turn of the twentieth century a programme was followed to make the tower safe, and the tower room visitable and furnished. The Town Council voted that the tower ought to be made presentable, appropriate relics ought to be

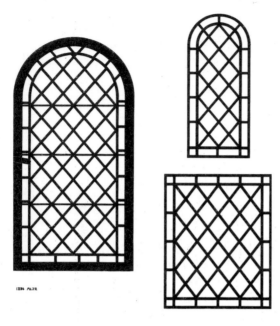

Fig. 72. Interior views of the three leaded windows. Left, the main north-eastern window; above right, the south-western attic window; and below right, the south-eastern stairway window.

placed therein, and the key kept nearby for public visits. This had been done by 1902. The furniture present today is but part of the accoutrements deposited then (Fig. 37). Two framed wash-drawings and a manuscript were hung on the wall under the wall-walk. The manuscript is an English transcript of the 1297 murage grant. The two wash-drawings, in pencil with a brown wash and white highlights, formerly framed together, have been attributed to Mary Bagnall-Oakeley. They are artist's impressions of Monnow Bridge's appearance in olden days. The first resembles the aquatint by John Ireland. The other view (Fig. 73) depicts the bridge before the gothic pedestrian passage was created. Strangely, a platform is indicated not to the passage but going all around the tower end.[158]

The displayed relics planned by the Town Council were housed here in the tower room. But, all have now vanished without trace; a fact that is not surprising considering that for many years the key was kept only yards from the bridge and it could be borrowed by anyone at any reasonable time. A list of these relics has not survived, although they are known to have included pieces of stone, some riddled with musket shot, removed from the tower during the then recent repairs.[159] A decade beforehand a hoard of Roman coins and an eighteenth-century pistol (Fig. 34) were found in the bed under the bridge, and these may have been part of the exhibits.

The furniture itself consists of a table, a chair, and a railed flight of steps. The source of the steps is not known, but both of the other pieces were donated as

Fig. 73. A wash-drawing of Monnow Bridge attributed to Mary Bagnall-Oakeley (1833–1904) that formerly hung in the tower room. At the bottom right corner in pencil is written, 'From an old sketch in possession of [illegible]'.

objects of appropriate antiquity and to add some comfort. The table is drop-leaved with an oval top that has the ends truncated. There are twisted legs and cross members. The chair is a wooden side chair, mostly of very plain carving, with a cloth upholstered seat. The back has a Cupid's bow top, and the splat is pierced with the fretworked design of a stylized lyre.[160]

Musket Holes

Along the front wall of the room there are two 'peep-holes' and a large central recess. The recess is the remainder of an arrow loop embrasure matching that one surviving at the head of the current stairway. Now, rather than a loop, it reveals the back of the exterior facework. Some engravings of the gate in the early 1800s indicate clearly some type of elongated opening at this point on the outer wall face. The embrasure and holes can be seen under the machicolation arches in the elevation drawing by John Carter of 1801 (Fig. 17), and the aquatint by Samuel Prout (Fig. 18) appears even to show a raked outer embrasure.

Until repairs by the County Council in 1982, this central internal recess also contained a peep-hole through the wall at the same height as the other two. The purpose of these holes is uncertain. Town guidebooks of the 1870s and later state that

on the western side of the gateway, under the arcade, appear several rough holes knocked through the wall; these were for musketry in anticipation of the advance of the Chartists on Monmouth County Gaol after their attack on Newport in 1839; the gateway would then have been an effective military post, for the river was not fordable, in consequence of the heavy rains which had delayed until daylight the entry of the Chartists into Newport, otherwise intended to have been effected at midnight.[161]

This account by Waugh is interesting but incorrect. Clearly he refers to the same holes, since no evidence remains that the wall was pierced anywhere else under the machicolation. Yet the holes are visible on engravings pre-dating 1839!

These three small loopholes have an uncertain former purpose. Since the wall at this point is 46 cm. thick, and the holes are completely straight, the view through them is quite distant (Fig. 74). They would be useless for firing upon attackers near to the tower, and it is difficult to imagine an attempt to aim or fire an arrow through them towards attackers as far distant as the present square. Their use for musketry, as suggested by Waugh, cannot be discounted. But, they certainly date from before 1800. A further possibility is that they are remaining putlog holes, that is, holes in which wooden scaffolding beams could be lodged. This possibility, though, is no more likely than that of musket loops. The tower is so compact that if putlogs were necessary it is hardly likely that they would

Fig. 74. View through the loophole under the north-western machicolation arch, 27 October 1985.

have been made over the road arch, not that high above the roadway. At present Waugh's purpose appears the most likely, except in his dating.

Putlog holes do appear to have existed on Monnow Gate at least until the cosmetic works of the late nineteenth century. In a water-colour painting by George Samuel, dated 1801, and the drawing by Munn (Fig. 14), a vertical row of regularly spaced putlog holes can be seen clearly over the river at the edge of the rounded downstream tower wall. Similarly, several conspicuous square holes existed amongst the ashlar blocks at the opposite side of the tower near the garderobe (Fig. 29).

Garderobe and Passage

At the end of the room are the ruined newel stair and the garderobe chamber (Fig. 75). Originally off the newel stair here was a vestibule presenting to the right a stone jambed and lintelled doorway leading into the garderobe chamber and to the left a doorway into the tower room(s). Only the right-hand jamb of this latter doorway survives. On the room side it is chamfered with plain stops at top and bottom. The former lintel has been cut off flush with the jamb, the inner face of which is damaged. Within the garderobe doorway, past the plain arrow slit the passage curves around the former newel stair, its outer wall making a projection from the rest of the tower. At the end there is a slight right-angled left turn making the top of the garderobe shaft. There would once have been a stone slab over the

Fig. 75. The garderobe passageway, 28 September 1988.

shaft forming a seat, but this has been removed. A decorative grille (Fig. 76) now covers the old shaft, down which one can see corbels supporting the structure and the river far below. The shaft, 122 cm in depth, discharged waste conveniently into the river. Now, though, the widened bridge and parapet blocks any outfall.

Fig. 76. Decorative grille covering the garderobe shaft.

Ruined Original Stair

The gate's stone newel stair survives in a ruinous condition for no apparent reason (Fig. 77). As noted above, the bottom portion was destroyed in order to build a passageway at road level. But, this does not explain why all of the upper steps have been hewn off.

The stone steps were wedge-shaped with a rounded portion at the narrow end. The broad end was built into the surrounding wall and the narrow end overlapped with others to create a continuous vertical newel post at the centre of the stairway. The steps all have a rise of around 16 cm., but, curiously, the circumferential run varies. The lower steps have a run of 33–4 cm., yet the mid-level ones have 60–6 cm. runs. When being built the stair had to pass an arrow slit embrasure and meet the upper floor at predetermined points. Variation in the run of steps may have been a clumsy method of matching the stairway to these critical points, or larger runs at the upper steps may indicate rebuilding of the upper stairway at some time.

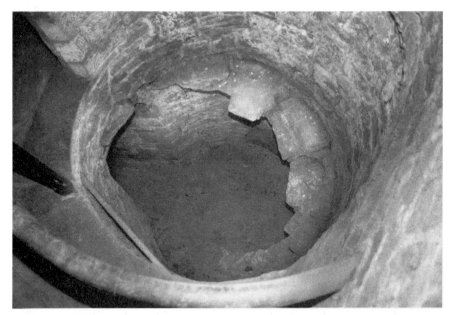

Fig. 77. Monnow Gate's ruined stone stairway, 28 September 1988.

The steps rise counterclockwise. This is unusual for a fortified building since in these it was customary for circular stairs to rise clockwise so that an ascending defender could have full use of the weapon in his right hand. The right-handed attacker would have difficulty in wielding his sword due to the newel post at his right. There are two factors which dictated the direction of turn when the gate was built, the position of the entrance door and the short length of the road passage side wall. When open the main road doors would have covered much of the adjacent side walls of the road passage. Thus, for the sake of convenience, the tower stair entrance had to be placed towards the rear of this passage. From such a point the compact size of the tower side dictated that the stair had to begin directly from the doorway, there being insufficient room for any significant vestibule or passage. Thus, the stair had to begin at the door and turn upward to the left. Leading on from this, placement of the stair dictated also that any cross arrow slit at the front of the building had to be placed in an embrasure opening off the stairway at a mezzanine level rather than at ground level.

Directly above the broken steps, a slight ridge in the masonry echoes the circular rise of the steps below. This may mark the position of the original ceiling of the stairway. Or, this ridge may represent a vestige of further steps which once continued up to the wall-walk.

Cross Arrow Slit Embrasure

Running obliquely off the stairway is the embrasure of the surviving cruciform arrow slit (Fig. 78). The obliqueness is in order to position the slit in the projecting wall adjacent to the road archway without causing any of the walls surrounding the passage to be too slender. The embrasure floor slopes downward slightly to the loop, and the massive weight above is carried on stepped lintels of full embrasure width.[162]

Cross arrow slits developed from plain slits early in the thirteenth century. The slit embrasure is necessarily small on the inside; too small to accommodate the width of a crossbow, and certainly too short to allow a six foot high longbow. Thus, defending archers are likely to have stood back at the stairs. With little change in embrasure design, the cross slit horizontal arms allowed the archer a much greater field of lateral vision without having to be positioned close to the loop. Viewed from inside, the right arm of the cross would appear unnecessary since attackers would most likely be on the bridge, i.e. in front or to the left. In fact, this arm was absent from all known illustrations of the gate until the arm was restored in the 1890s. At other medieval fortifications three-armed cross slits are uncommon. A similar cruciform loop at the Water Tower, Kenilworth Castle, has little apparent need for the right cross arm due to a wall directly to the right of the stair turret off which three cross loops are situated. The loop is three-armed, with the right one absent. However, exterior examination shows that the right arm is present but filled in. The other two loops above remain four-armed. It is probable that originally Monnow Gate's cross was complete also.

Alure and Machicolation

Moving back up to the room, we continue with the alure (Fig. 71), that wide ledge at the front of the room. As noted above, this wall-walk was originally exterior to the tower room. The low-pitched roof ran from its inner edge to the wall opposite. Access was probably from the newel stairway or from a ladder up through a trapdoor. At this point the present front wall was a battlemented parapet with the low portions (crenels) perhaps reaching to waist level and the tall portions (merlons) being slightly higher than a man's height. The merlons may have possessed arrow loops so that a defender could fire upon the enemy without having to expose himself by standing at a crenel.

At the front centre of the alure are the three machicolation chutes. Now they are guarded by metal bars, but originally they would have been open or would have had removable covers. Through the chutes the machicolation arches can be seen, as well as the portcullis grooves and the main arch where the roadway doors once hung. A defender at the alure could employ the machicolation when attackers had weathered the fusillade from the various loops. The enemy that had reached the gate could still be repulsed by fire from directly above, and water could be thrown down if the enemy attempted to burn the gates. There are tales of molten oil or lead being poured down upon the foe. But, lead seems rather a dear commodity to dispose of so lightly.

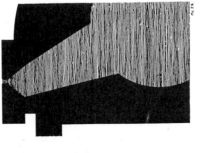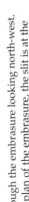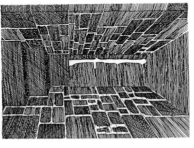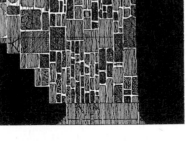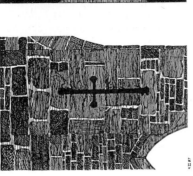

Fig. 78. Drawings of the cross arrow slit embrasure. From the left: exterior elevation; section through the embrasure looking north-west. the arrow slit is to the left, the stairway is to the right; view of the embrasure from the stairway; plan of the embrasure, the slit is at the top, the stairwell is at the bottom right.

Attic and Roof

As outlined above, when the gate was made into a dwelling, the wall-walk level was remodelled as an attic room. The battlement was partly rebuilt as solid wall, the attic window was inserted, and an enlarged roof with a dormer was added (Fig. 79).

The roof beams rest in the wall at just below the top of the old parapet. The three main trusses would have been placed across with a ridge piece to hold them upright. Iron bars from the ends of the tie beams at the bottom of the trusses continue across the wall and loop over the outside face. Half-way up the trusses two trenched through purlin beams rest on each side to support the common rafters. At the ends of the tower, where the roof is round, the rafters spray out umbrella-like and their tops are given further support by a beam placed obliquely, its end standing upon the adjacent tie beam (Fig. 80). The roundness makes it difficult to employ purlins here, so several of the rafters are supported from below by struts which rest on horizontal beams let into each end wall. A small number of the existing timbers have been reused.

The rafters begin up at the ridge piece, pass down over the purlins, and rest at the bottom end over a wall-plate on the outer side of the wall top. Since behind

Fig. 79. Interior of the roof looking south-east, 21 March 1992.

the wall-plate there is a triangular space under the rising rafters, on this side the wall was continued upward in brick. Thus, the bottom of the brick infill marks wall-plate level.

Over the common rafters, battens are attached upon which the tilestones are hung. Since the tiles decrease in size towards the apex, the battens also become closer. Joints where the tiles overlap are sealed on the inner side by a rendering at the tops of the exposed tiles called torching.

Fig. 80. North-western end of the roof viewed from the ruined stairway, 21 March 1992. One of the tower tie rods can be seen (bottom left), as well as the alure ledge.

Appendices

APPENDIX A

Extract from a Patent Roll of 25 Edward I, dated 27 August, 1297.

Text within square brackets indicates the beginning point of lines in the original manuscript, or comment.

[Margin] Murage for the Town of Monmouth
[1] The King to the Bailiffs and honest men of Monmouth greeting. Know that at the instance of Henry of Lancaster, our well beloved nephew, and your lord, we have granted to you in aid of enclosing the town aforesaid, [2] and for the greater security of these parts, that from the day of the completion of these present to the end of five years next following fully completed you may levy in the same [3] town of each quarter of corn for sale, one obol. Of each horse and mare, ox and cow for sale, one obol. For each hide of horse and mare, ox [4] and cow, fresh, salted, or tanned for sale one farthing. For each cart carrying meat salted, or fresh for sale, three obols. For five fat hogs [5] for sale, one obol. For ten young pigs for sale, one obol. For each fresh salmon for sale, one farthing. For each lamprey for sale before Easter one [6] farthing. For ten sheep, goats, or pigs for sale one penny. For ten fleeces, for sale, one obol. For one hundred skins of wooled sheep, goats, [7] red deer stags and hinds, and fallow deer stags and hinds for sale, one penny. For each hundred skins of lambs, kids, hares, rabbits, foxes, cats, and [8] squirrels for sale, one obol. For each cartload of salt for sale, one penny. For each quarter of salt for sale one farthing. For each quarter of flour [9] beans and peas for sale one farthing. For each horse-load of pieces of cloth for sale, one obol. For each whole piece of cloth for sale, one obol. For each hundred of linen yarn [10] hundred of cloth of Ireland, Wales, and worsted for sale, one obol. For each piece of cloth of silk with gold of samite, diaper and Baudekyn for sale [11] one obol. For each piece of cloth of silk without gold and mixed Cendal, for sale, one farthing. For each ship coming to the town [12] by water carrying goods for sale, three pence. For each horse-load of sea fish for sale one obol. For each cask of wine and ashes for sale, three obols.

For each [13] horse-load of ashes for sale, one obol. For each horse-load of honey for sale one penny. For each cask of honey for sale, three pence. For each bag of wool for sale, four [14] pence. For each bale of pieces of rag for sale, drawn by cart, two pence. For each horse-load of cloth for sale, or other diverse and small articles to be sold, [15] coming to the same town one obol. For each cartload of iron for sale one penny. For each cartload of lead for sale two pence. For each horse-load of tan [16] for sale, per week, one obol. Of timber by weight, namely of one hundred, one penny. For each pot of pitch and oil for sale one penny. For each quarter of Whey [?] [17] for sale, two pence. For each hundred of Alum, and Copper for sale one obol. For two thousand onions for sale one farthing. For each horse-load of garlic [18] for sale one obol. For each thousand of herrings for sale one farthing. For each hundred of boards for sale one obol. For each millstone for sale [one?] obol. For each wey of cheese [19] and Butter for sale, one obol. For each dozen horse-loads of coal for sale, one obol. For each cartload of firewood for sale per week, one obol. [20] For each horse-load of firewood for sale, per week one farthing. For each thousand nails for the roofs of houses for sale one farthing. For each [21] hundred shoes for horses, and clouts for carts, for sale, one obol. For two thousand of various nails, except for nails for carts, and for the roofs of [22] houses, for sale, one farthing. For each bale of miscellaneous wares, to be sold at the said town, and exceeding the value of two shillings, one [23] farthing. For each hundred of tin, brass, and copper for sale two pence. For each hundred bars of steel for sale, one obol. For each ship laden with [24] turf, lime, and sparstone for sale, two pence. For each hundred of Aberdeen [fish] for sale, one penny. For each hundred of stockfish for sale one obol. For [25] ten stone of hemp for sale one farthing. For ten gallons of oil for sale, one obol. For each cauldron and lead vessel for sale for brewing, one obol. For each hundred of salmon, [26] mullets, congers and sea urchins, and salted eels for sale one penny. And therefore we command you to levy the said customs to the end of the term aforesaid, as aforesaid but at [27] the completion of the said term of five years the said customs will wholly cease and be abolished. In testimony of which, for the aforesaid five years, witness as above by the King himself before his transfretation.

This is a revised translation from the original manuscript after reference to the editions of E.H. Culley in Bagnall-Oakeley (1896) and Kissack in Kissack (1974).

APPENDIX B

Conveyance of Monnow Gate to Messrs Rosser, Bibee, and Bibee, dated 20 November 1705.

Text within square brackets indicates the beginning point of lines in the original manuscript, or comment. Spellings and abbreviations are left unchanged, but obsolete abbreviation marks are replaced by apostrophes.

[1] **This Indenture** Made the Twentieth day of November in the foureth yeare of the Reigne of our Sovereigne Lady Anne by the Grace of God of England Scotland France and Ireland [2] Queene Defender of the Faith et' Anno' Dm. 1705 **Betweene** Henry Barnes Esq. Mayor of the Towne and Burrough of Monmouth Thomas Bellamy and Thomas Woodward Gentlemen Bayliffes of the [3] said Towne and Burrough of Monmouth and the whole Com'onalty of the said Towne and Burrough of the one parte And Roger Rosser of the Towne of Monmouth aforesaid Carpenter Mathew Bibee and Henry Bibee Two of [4] the sonnes of James Bibee of the Towne aforesaid Innholder of the other parte **Witnesseth** That the said Mayor Bayliffes and Com'onalty with one Consent Assent and mutuall agreement for and in Considerat'on [5] of the Rent and Covenants hereafter in and by these presents reserved expressed and comprized **have** demised granted and to Farme letten And by these presents Do demise grant and to Farme lett and sett [6] unto the said Roger Rosser Mathew Bibee and Henry Bibee **All** That peece of building comonly called Monow gate Situate on Monnow Bridge within the said Towne and the Office of Porter of the [7] said Gate together with all advantages perquisites and emoluments whatsoever thereto belonging or appertaining **To have and to hold** all and singular the premisses hereby demised or [8] ment'oned to be demised with the Apptenances unto the said Roger Rosser Mathew Bibee and Henry Bibee from the day of the date of these presents for and dureing the Termes of their naturall lives [9] successively and the life and lives of the Survivor and Survivors of them successively and to the assignee and assignes of the Survivor and Survivors of them and every of them successively **yeildinge** and [10] paying therefore yearly and for every year during the said Terme unto the said Mayor Bayliffes and Com'onalty their Successors and assignes into the Chamber of the said Towne the Rent or Sume of [11] one Shilling of Lawful money of England at or upon the Feast of Saint Michael the Archangell yearly dureing the said Terme And also one Couple of fat Capons to the Mayor of the said Towne [12] for the time being at every the Feast of the Nativity of our Blessed Lord and Saviour Jesus Christ dureing the said Terme **provided** always and upon Condit'on That if the said yearly Rent and Capons [13] shall be behind and unpaid in parte or in all upon the said Feast dayes on which the same ought to be respectively paid as aforesaid being Lawfully demanded and no sufficient distresse to be found on the [14] premisses That then it shall and may be Lawfull to and for the said Mayor Bayliffes and Com'onalty their Heires and Successors into the premisses hereby granted and every parte and parcell thereof [15] with th apptenances to Reenter and the same to have againe Repossesse and enjoy as his and their former Estate Anything herein contained to the contrary in any wise notwithstanding **And** the said [16] Roger Rosser for himselfe and the said Mathew Bibee and Henry Bibee his Executors adm' and assignes doth by these presents Covenant promise and grant to and with the said Mayor Bayliffes and [17] Comonalty their Successors and assignes in manner and forme following That is to say That he the said Roger Rosser Mathew Bibee and Henry Bibee their Exto' adm' and assignes [18] shall and will well and truely pay or cause to be

paid the said yearly Rent and Capons before reserved unto the said Mayor Bayliffes and Com'onalty and his and their successors and [19] assignes yearly dureing the said Terme upon the dayes and times before limitted for payment thereof **And** also that he the said Roger Rosser his Exto' Adm' and assignes [20] shall and will at his and their proper Costs and Charges within the space of Twelve moneths now next ensueing Convert the said Gate into a good and sufficient dwelling house [21] and shall make two good roomes in the first floore one story high and shall convert the other Floore into Garretts or roomes and cover the same with Tile stones **And** further alsoe [22] That he the said Roger Rosser Mathew Bibee and Henry Bibee and their severall and respective Exto' Adm' and assignes shall and will from time to time and at all times hereafter dureing [23] the said Terme when and as often as need shall require well and sufficiently maintaine repair uphold and keep as well the premisses hereby granted with the Apptenances as also such roomes [24] and bulding as the said Roger Rosser shall build thereupon as aforesaid in and with all and all manner of needfull and necessary reparat'ons and amendments whatsoever and at the end of the [25] said Terme shall quietly and peaceably leave and yeild up the said premisses unto the said Mayor Bayliffes and Com'onalty their Successors and assignes in all respects Tenantable **And** the [26] said Mayor Bayliffes and Com'onalty for themselves their Successors and assignes do by these presents Covenant and grant to and with the said Roger Rosser Mathew Bibee and Henry Bibee their [27] and either of their assignes That they the said Roger Rosser Mathew Bibee and Henry Bibee and their respective assignes paying the yearely rent afore reserved and performing the Covenants and agreements [28] herein contained on his and their partes and behalfes to be kept observed and performed shall and may peaceably and quietly have hold and enjoy the p'misses hereby granted with the Appurtenances [29] during the said Terme without the let suite molestat'on or interrupt'on of the said Mayor Bayliffes and Com'onalty their Successors or assignes or of any other person or persons lawfully clayming from by [30] or under them or any of them **In Witnesse** whereof to the one parte of this p'sent Indenture remaining with the said Roger Rosser The said Mayor Bayliffes and Comonalty have caused the Com'on [31] seale of the said Towne to be affixed the day month and year first above written.
[32] Sealed and Delivered, and peaceable and quiet possion' [33] and Livery and Seisin of the Premisses above ment'oned [34] to be grannted, duely made given and executed by the abovenam'd [35] Mayor Bayliffes and Com'onalty of the said Towne of Monmouth [36] unto the said Roger Rosser for his own use as also for the use [37] of the said Mathew Bybee and Henry Bibee according to the true [38] Intent and meaning of this p'sent Indenture in the presence of

[signed] [39] Parker Bohune
  [40] Cha. Gwyn.

Transcription from the original indented manuscript on heavy paper in the Monmouth Borough Archives.

Glossary

Terms are explained only with reference to contexts in this book.

Abacus – a flat slab which forms the top of a capital.

Alure – walkway along the top of a wall, usually behind a parapet wall.

Arch ring – a series of voussoirs making an arch, or one of several arches of voussoirs projecting below a wider arch.

Ashlar – masonry hewn with even faces and square edges, usually laid in horizontal courses with thin joints.

Battlement – a defensive parapet with alternate indentations (crenels) and raised portions (merlons).

Baudekyn – a rich fabric, originally woven with woof of silk and warp of gold.

Borough – a town which has a corporation and privileges conferred by royal charter.

Cames – the H-shaped lead strips which secure individual panes in a leaded window.

Cendal – a thin rich silken material.

Centring – a temporary curved wooden framework upon which an arch or vault is built.

Chamberlain – the treasurer of a corporation.

Chamfer – a slanted surface made on a block of stone or wood when a 90° edge is cut away to form two obtuse edges.

Chats – ore with matrix still adhering.

Clout – a nail with a large flat head.

Commonalty – the people of a town, a corporate body.

Coping – stones laid to protect the top of a wall.

Corbel – a block of stone part of which projects from a wall, the projection used for support.

Corvizer – cordwainer, shoemaker.

Cutwater – wedge-shaped end of a bridge pier.

Diaper – a fabric with lines crossing diamond-wise, the spaces filled by decoration.

Embrasure – an opening in a wall or parapet for a door or window, usually splayed on the inside.

Extrados – the outer or convex face of an arch.

Falsework – a temporary framework used during building, centring.

Farthing – former British currency unit, a quarter of a penny.

Garderobe – a term applied to medieval lavatories and wardrobes.

Gout – a drain or culvert.

Green glass – a coarse glass of green colour, bottle glass.

Half-pace – a raised floor or platform, or a staircase landing.

Intrados – the inner or concave face of an arch.

Jamb – the vertical face of an archway or doorway.

Joint – the space between blocks of wall masonry.

Lintel – a horizontal beam or stone over an aperture.

Lock-up – a room or building used for the temporary detention of prisoners.

Machicolation – a parapet or gallery projecting out from a wall on brackets between which are holes through which missiles or water can be thrown down.

Mercer – dealer in textile fabrics.

Metalling – road-metal, broken stones, etc., used as a road surface.

Micaceous – made of or containing the mineral mica.

Murage – a tax levied for the building of town walls.

Newel – the post supporting the ends of treads of a wooden circular stair, or the narrow, rounded ends of steps forming with their neighbours the central post of stone circular stairs.

Obol – former British currency unit, half of a penny.

Oillet – round hole occurring along or at the end of an arrow loop.

Ordnance datum – mean sea-level as defined by the Ordnance Survey.

Parapet – a wall built at the edge of a roof or bridge.

Portcullis – a heavy defensive gate often shod with iron which can slide up and down in grooves.

Purlin – a beam laid across principal rafters to support the common rafters.

Quarry – a diamond-shaped glass pane.

Rubble – rough unhewn building stones that are not normally laid in regular courses.

Samite – a rich silk fabric, sometimes interwoven with gold.

Shilling – former British currency unit, abbreviated as *s*. 1*s*. (shilling) = 12*d*. (old pence) = 5p (new pence) = 1/20 of one pound.

Soffit – the under-surface of an arch or lintel, the intrados.

Sole plate – a sill, or the lowest horizontal member of a framed construction.

Spandrel – walling at the side of an arch, bound by the extrados and two imaginary lines, one line running horizontally through the crown of the extrados and the other running vertically through the extrados at the arch's springing point.

Springing stone (springer) – the stone that begins an arch, or, strictly, that end arch stone with a horizontal face bedded in the supporting wall.

Stallage – rent or toll taken in exchange for the right to erect a market stall.

String – a sloping board, the vertical face of which carries the treads and risers of a staircase.

String course – a horizontal band of stones projecting from a wall, often decorative.

Tell-tale – device attached across an existing crack or joint in a wall to monitor any movement of one side relative to the other.

Transfretation – crossing of a strait or narrow sea.

Voussoir – a squared building stone with two opposite converging sides, used with others to form an arch.

Wall-plate – a horizontal beam at the top of a wall that carries rafters or joists.

Wall-walk – a walkway at the top of a wall, often positioned behind a parapet.

Wey – an archaic unit of weight or volume varying in size according to the commodity.

Notes

Source Abbreviations

Beacon – *Monmouthshire Beacon* newspaper
Cadw – Cadw: Welsh Historic Monuments
GCCCES – Gwent County Council, County Engineer and Surveyor's Department
GCRO – Gwent County Record Office
GGAT – Glamorgan-Gwent Archaeological Trust
MAS – Monmouth Archaeological Society
MBA – Monmouth Borough Archives (i.e. archives of the pre-1974 Borough of Monmouth, not of the Monmouth Borough Council created in 1988)
MBC – Monmouth Borough Council (created in August 1988)
MDC – Monmouth District Council (renamed MBC in August 1988)
Merlin – *Monmouthshire Merlin* newspaper
MLJR – the author
NLW – National Library of Wales
NMR – National Monuments Record for Wales
SWHP – Sir William Halcrow and Partners Ltd.
WWA – Welsh Water Authority

1   Excavation has suggested that in Roman times the area bordering Monnow Street was laid out as fields; the Roman artefacts being in the form of pottery, metalwork, and coins. The first structural remains from the street, i.e. evidence of dwellings, do not occur until late in the eleventh century, soon after the founding of Monmouth Castle (Clarke 1987a, 1989; GGAT 1987; MAS 1989, 1991a; *South Wales Argus*, 'Scientist backs date of town's ancient house', 2 September 1988).

2   Hardy 1833.

3   Wendover in Hewlett 1886–9. Paris in Luard 1876.

4   Kissack 1974. Dew and Wood in the work *Notes on Monmouth*, an undated typescript by E.N. Dew at Monmouth Museum.

5   Grose 1773–87. Beattie 1842.

6   Taylor 1951. Kissack 1974.

7   MAS 1991b.

8   PRO: Patent roll 25 Edward I, pt. 2, memb. 6, C66/117. Turner 1971. Barley 1975.

9   Turner 1971. PRO: Patent roll 8 Edward II, pt. 2, memb. 6, C66/143. The text of the 1315 grant is similar though considerably shorter than that of 1297.

10   West Gate is the only gate about which there are doubts of its existence. John
        Speed's otherwise detailed and reasonably accurate town view of 1610 does not
        include West Gate. Neither does it indicate the ditch running across south of the
        town. However, a drawbridge at that site is referred to in a Civil War account. 'The
        Enemy no sooner espied him [Lt.Col. Kyrle] approaching with 100 Muskettiers, but
        they presently retreated to the lower end of Monnow street and upon his comming
        to the inmost Bridge in the midst of Monnow street he commanded it to be let
        down' (Transcription of letter dated 4 Feb. 1645 in Webb and Webb 1879).
            Archaeological evidence has been found adjacent to the present road of a large
        wooden structure that overlooked the ditch (a defensive building/gate?)
        apparently erected in the late eleventh century and removed in the next century
        (MAS 1991a).

11   Leland in Hearne 1769 and Smith 1964. Camden in Camden 1735.
            Leland mentions both Wye Gate and Monnow Gate. Only for the latter does he
        emphasize that it is actually on the bridge. The former is likely to have been on
        land adjacent to the Wye Bridge.
            Recent excavations – Mrs Bagnall-Oakeley (1896) makes observations on
        defensive features then visible. Excavation in 1973 found evidence of the northern
        rampart and ditch (Shoesmith 1990). In a 1984 excavation in the cellar at the corner
        of Nailer's Lane/Monnow Street (i.e. 25 Monnow Street) MAS found evidence of
        the ditch in line with Nailer's Lane (*Monmouth Archaeology* 17:6). In 1987 at Burton
        Homes, Glendower Street, groundwork for a new building revealed the town ditch
        to a depth of 3.8 m. (Clarke 1987b). A further ditch, 8 m. wide and 3.5 m. deep, has
        been found also running obliquely from the south ditch in the direction of the
        castle; the infill containing thirteenth-century pottery (*Beacon* 17 May 1991, 8 April
        1993; MAS 1991a, MAS 1991b).

12   Figs. 3 and 27 are based upon three types of evidence used in following order of
        precedence – evidence still embodied in the building, evidence about the gate from
        contemporary documents and illustrations, and practices and designs employed on
        other comparable buildings of the time.
            Surviving medieval portcullises and winding mechanisms are uncommon in Britain,
        most portcullis equipment having been destroyed long ago. An impressive original
        portcullis and mechanism exists at Hever Castle in Kent. Sandwiched between two
        walls, it is hung on two chains passing up over a windlass and then down inside the
        gateway rooms to end with massive lead weights. Sixteenth-century replacement
        mechanisms survive at the thirteenth-century Byward and Bloody Towers at the
        Tower of London, and at the keep of Arundel Castle are a small portcullis and winch.
        In South Wales there are reconstructed mechanisms at Manorbier Castle, St Donat's
        Castle, and at Castell Coch. A flimsy reconstructed portcullis can be seen at Caerphilly
        Castle. At St Donat's the early fourteenth-century outer gatehouse has a modern
        counterweight which greatly assists in raising the massive gate. Similarly, in the
        restoration (1875–91) of Castell Coch by William Burges *et al.* there is an arrangement
        whereby a counterweight is employed along with counterbalancing of the portcullis
        and drawbridge. Viollet-le-Duc's *magnum opus* shows the designs of other
        counterweighted mechanisms (Viollet-le-Duc 1854–68).

13   White Castle (Radford 1982, Knight 1992), Chepstow Castle (Perks 1967, Knight
        1986), Caerphilly Castle (Johns 1978, Renn 1989), Usk Castle (Knight 1977), St
        Donat's Castle (Reid 1983), Carisbrooke Castle (Peers 1982).

Kenilworth Castle (Toy 1939, Thompson 1977, 1991). The lowest of the three cross arrow loops at the Water Tower, Kenilworth Castle, has a striking similarity to the one at Monnow Gate in size, embrasure layout, depth, and position on a stairway. Here the stair is intact and the embrasure bed has not been altered.

Leybourne Castle (Toy 1939, Renn 1981). Eight well-preserved cruciform slits or ruined slits survive on the gatehouse at Leybourne. However, an engraving after Badeslade (in Harris 1719) and other eighteenth-century engravings suggest that several of the existing loops are not original.

Oillets designed for guns generally vary from 13 cm. to 31 cm. in width. For example, at the inner gatehouse of Cooling Castle, gun loops dating from 1381 have oillet diameters of 20 cm. Loops of comparable date at Canterbury's West Gate have 25 cm. oillets (O'Neill 1960, Nichols 1979, Bowen 1982, Renn 1982).

Research into the use and effectiveness of arrow loops was carried out at White Castle by Jones and Renn (1982).

14   Radford 1952.

15   King 1988. Toy 1939.

The ring of beam holes without corbelling seen on the Garrison Tower of Usk Castle is somewhat below the parapet since the height of the tower was raised subsequently (Knight 1977).

16   Carmarthen, Llawhaden, and Kidwelly Castles in Colvin 1963, James 1980, Kenyon 1986, Radford 1952, Radford 1980. Cooling Castle in Harris 1910, Nichols 1979. Scotney Castle in National Trust 1992. Hever Castle in Newman 1976, Watson 1984. Bodiam Castle in Curzon 1926, Morton 1981. Caldicot Castle in Birbeck 1973. Leeds Castle in Wykeham-Martin 1869, Newman 1976, and Anon. 1989. Carisbrooke Castle in O'Neill 1960 and Peers 1982. Others in Turner 1971, Viollet-le-Duc 1854–68, Chatelain 1987.

17   Monmouth charter of Henry VI, PRO: DL 37/15 No. 27. Transcript in MBA: K.E. Kissack, *Monmouth Documents and Charters* I:404–8.

18   The Monmouth charter of 3 Edward VI survives in various forms in the MBA. There is an original manuscript copy on parchment, a differing Latin transcription (MBA: Historical Evidence), a translation by John Hobson Matthews (MBA: Monmouth Records III), and a different translation (MBA: Historical Evidence).

19   The town clerk's view comes from his letter of 16 September 1819 regarding the history of Monmouth Town Gaol. MBA: Gaol 1811–20 No.8.

20   Charter of 4 James I (1607). Transcription and translation by E.N. Dew in MBA: Monmouth Charters.

Charter of 17 Charles I (1641). Transcription and translation in MBA: Monmouth Charters.

21   MBA: Transcript by J.H. Matthews of case and counsel's opinion dated 19 January 1705. MBA: Common Council Minutes 5 May 1705. Bradney 1907a.

If Moore Price was coming to Monmouth from Llanvihangel Ysterne Llewerne, then it is peculiar that this episode occurred at Wye Bridge rather than Monnow Bridge.

22   MBA: Monmouth Documents and Charters IV; R and V 1782/1783 No.10; John Middleton's Accounts for 1714; Misc. 1811–20 No.1.

23   'Monmoth Castell . . . is nowe and hath byn for a longe tyme altogether Ruynous and in decaye . . . havinge one greate hall which is covered and maynteyned for the Judges of Assisses to sitt in.' Transcript from part of a survey of the Duchy of Lancaster in 1610 (Rees 1953).

24   Phillips 1874.

25   Webb and Webb 1879. Another (contemporary) account transcript in Phillips 1874.

26   From the transcript of a letter by C.H. dated 4 February 1645 in Webb and Webb 1879.

27   Bradney 1907b. *Beacon* 9 July 1859. Heath 1804.

28   MBA: Common Council Minutes 8 October 1705.

29   MBA: Conveyances 1700-10 No. 9.

30   MBA: Historical Evidence; Quarter Sessions Proceedings dates – 6 April 1719, 21 October 1723, 18 January 1725, October 1725, 24 October 1728, January 1731, 10 January 1732, 16 January 1738.

31   MBA: Common Council Minutes 4 February 1706, incorrectly written as 1705 in the original manuscript.

32   MBA: Accounts 1700–39.

33   MBA: Accounts 1700–39, 'Mr John Middleton's Acct. of Stewardship for 1714'. Summary of Henry Barnes lease in Monmouth Documents and Charters III, and Accounts 1700–39 No. 3.

34   MBA: Monmouth Borough Council Minutes 14 September 1730; Accounts 1700–39 No. 5 'John Middleton's Rents for 1729'. GCRO: D10.2476, the will of Henry Barnes.

35   St Stephen's Gate was converted to the town gaol in 1710. The lease to Thomas Williams has conditions that are very similar to the 1705 Monnow Gate lease. MBA: Monmouth Borough Council Minutes 8 October 1705, 29 October 1705; Monmouth Records VIII 5 August 1710.

        MBA: Monmouth Borough Quarter Sessions Proceedings 20 April 1723, 10 January 1732; Minutes of the Common Council 27 October 1768; Monmouth Documents and Charters IV; R and V 1782/1783 No. 60. Kissack 1991.

36   MBA: R and V 1766/1767 No.35, and transcription in Monmouth Records.

37   MBA: R and V 1768/1769 No. 10; R and V 1771 No. 19; R and V 1773 No. 26, No. 33; R and V 1774/1775 No. 33; F and D 1771–80 No. 26, No. 33.

38   MBA: Monmouth Documents and Charters III; R and V 1763 No. 14; R and V 1764 No. 23; R and V 1766/1767 No. 9; R and V 1771/1772 No. 20; R and V 1775 No. 9; R and V 1782/1783 No. 52, No. 60; R and V 1794 No. 3, No. 21, No. 22, No. 47; R and V 1800 No. 11; R and V 1804 No. 23; R and V 1809 No. 44.

39   MBA: R and V 1771 No. 19; R and V 1771/1772 No. 13, No. 29; R and V 1773 No. 11, No. 26, No. 27, No. 29, No. 33; R and V 1774 No. 11; R and V 1774/1775 No. 33. GCRO: D10/1.333.

40   MBA: R and V 1773 No. 28.

41   MBA: R and V 1773 No. 31, No. 32, No. 34.

42   MBA: R and V 1771/1772 No. 24, No. 25, No. 35; R and V 1773 No. 19, No. 20, No. 21.

43   MBA: R and V 1782/1783 No. 26, No. 28, No. 61, No. 62.

44   MBA: Monmouth Records VII; Proceedings of the Monmouth Borough Quarter Sessions 14 July 1788. Andrews 1890.

45   MBA: Proceedings of the Monmouth Borough Quarter Sessions 18 January 1790.

46   MBA: Mayor's notebook of cases brought before magistrates 1853–6.

47   Gilpin 1782.

48   Gilpin 1782. Heath 1808. Miles 1898.

49   The original sketch attributed to Grose, later engraved in his *Antiquities*, is at the Society of Antiquaries of London.

        The soft ground etching by John Sell Cotman (1782-1842) (see page 152), published in Cotman 1838, is a view from the site of the present cattle market. He visited Monmouth in the first days of July 1800 (Rajnai and Allthorpe-Guyton 1979, Moore 1982). There exists a water-colour drawing similar to the etching, dated 1802.

50 Three Monnow Bridge engravings after Samuel Prout's sketches appear in his *Rudiments of Landscape* (Prout 1813–14). They originate from Prout's tour of South Wales in 1813. Plate 46 is a view of the entire bridge from the south. As issued, the colouring imitates the appearance of a sketch of brown washes. The view of the gate, plate 59, is slightly more elaborate, with highlights of other colours. Plate 64 is in full colour. Prout's original water-colour painting for Plate 64 survives in the Paul Mellon Collection at the Yale Center for British Art.

A drain here adjacent to the bridge was, and remains, a frequent cause of troubles (*Beacon* 22 June 1990, 29 November 1991). The original was stone-built, emerging from Monnow Street and eventually plunging down the river bank to curve downstream into the river (MBA: Minutes of the Monmouth Paving Act 9 November 1818). The cattle market wall was erected over it creating an artificial division between land and water. Until the 1988/1990 flood works a disarticulated portion of this drain remained *in situ* on the river bed.

A fascinating bill dated 16 October 1809 (MBA: B and P 1809 No. 5) decrees that the drain should be maintained at the expense of the Corporation.

Estimates were supplied for repairs to the ancient drain in 1836 and 1837 (MBA: P and L 1836 No. 26, P and L 1837/1838 No. 5).

51 MBA: R and V 1812/1814 No. 86, No. 107; R and V 1815/1816 No. 3, No. 6, No. 17, No. 44, No. 80.

52 MBA: *An Act for Paving the Footways, and cleansing, lighting, and watching the Streets, in the Town of Monmouth.* The Act is summarized in Heath 1818. *Merlin* 23 and 30 May 1835, Municipal Corporation Report.

53 MBA: R and V 1818/1819 No. 16, No. 33, No. 43; Misc. 1811–20 No. 11.

54 MBA: R and V 1818/1819 No. 43, No. 49, No. 59; R and V 1819/1820 No. 2, No. 21, No. 28; R and V 1822 No. 14, No. 20; Corporation Account Book 1805–31.

55 MBA: R and V 1819/1820 No. 27, No. 48, No. 54; R and V 1822 No. 9, No. 14, No. 18, No. 22; R and V 1823 No. 5; Accounts 1821–30, 1822 Chamberlain's Accounts. GCRO: D361 F/P Misc 1.

56 GCRO: D10/1/36; D10/1/62. MBA: Corporation Rent Book 1831; Misc. 1830 No. 7, No. 8; Monmouth Borough Council Minutes 29 March 1830, 12 October 1830.

A water-colour by T.E. Rosenberg (see page viii), dated 1831, and a drawing by A.F. Wood, at NLW, show the new downstream widening as viewed from the churchyard. The Rosenberg painting also indicates that the Monnow Gate roof was in decay.

57 County of Monmouth 1844, 1857. *Beacon* 17 April 1852, 19 March 1853, 21 October 1876. GCRO: QSCofPC 9.34, letter to A. Waddington, Usk, from Charles Marriott dated 22 September 1845; QSPR 16.19 2 January 1843; QSPR 39.9 29 June 1863; QSPR 93.4 10 March 1877; QS.RB2 31 December 1838, 15 October 1838; QS.RB3 17 October 1842, 2 January 1843; QS.RB4 1 July 1844; QS.RB7 17 October 1859, 30 December 1861, 27 June 1864; QS.RB10 15 October 1878; QS.RB11 16 October 1883.

58 GCRO: QS.RB4 30 December 1844, 27 March 1845.

59 MBA: Minutes of the Common Council 12 October 1830. GCRO: D10.1280.

60 *Western Mail* 28 July 1887. *Merlin* 2 July 1831.

61 *Beacon* 30 June 1838.

62   *Merlin* 21 August 1847. *Beacon* 28 August 1847.

63   *Beacon* 2 May and 9 May 1891, 2 November 1900. Water-colours exist of the York visit, including a view of the decorated bridge.

64   *Beacon* 10 September 1881.

65   *Beacon* 9 February, 9 March, and 10 August 1900. GCRO: Mon. C.C. M.B. 1894–1900 7 February 1900.

66   *Beacon* 9 June 1883, 11 August 1883. The gate was retiled at this time. Before the work the tilestones had been generally larger than at present, with fewer courses which decreased less in size towards the ridge.

67   *Beacon* 12 January 1889, 16 November 1889. GCRO: C.R+B.M. 23 November 1889.

68   A photograph by Francis Frith (Frith negative 28782) shows the state of the structure in 1891. The new paving and guttering can be seen as well as the brace plates.

69   *Beacon* 19 March 1892, 23 April 1892, 7 May 1892. GCRO: C.R+B.M.1. 7 April 1892.

70   *Beacon* 6 August 1892.

71   *Beacon* 14 May 1892, 11 June 1892, 6 August 1892.

72   The pistol and corbel are preserved at Monmouth Museum.
      A bull of Urban III gives the list of Monmouth Priory possessions in 1186 (Kissack 1974, Round 1899).

73   Lecture Book No. 1 by F. Tyler-Taylor at Monmouth Museum.

74   GCRO: C.R+B.M. 13 October 1892. *Beacon* 5 November 1892, 5 August 1893.

75   GCRO: C.R+B.M. 13 April 1893. *Beacon* 15 April 1893.

76   *Beacon* 18 March 1988, 1 June 1990, 8 March 1991, 5 April 1991, 5 July 1991, 26 July 1991, 9 August 1991. *South Wales Argus* 24 May 1990.

77   *Beacon* 19 August 1893.
      Two surviving photographs of *circa* 1896 show Monnow Gate with new guttering and downpipes, fresh pointing, a new stone at the right of the cross arrow loop, and no glazing. These views are a photograph in the 1895–7 album of Eleanor Rolls (at Monmouth Museum) and a photograph at the NMR (negative 871157/6).

78   *Beacon* 10 November 1899, 9 February 1900, 9 March 1900, 6 April 1900.

79   *Beacon* 9 May 1902.
      A photograph of the newly refurbished gate, dated 1901 or 1902, by James Watts, appears in *Pilgrimages to Old Homes mostly on the Welsh Border* by Fletcher Moss 1903.

80   GCRO: Mon. C.C. M.B. 7 May 1902, 15 May 1902, 5 November 1902. The first *Monnow Bridge Tower Visitors' Book* is at Monmouth Museum. *Beacon* 21 November 1902, 12 December 1902.

81   GCRO: Mon. C.C. M.B. 1900–8 4 February 1903. Bagnall-Oakeley 1896, 1903.

82   *Beacon* 30 May 1986.

83   *Beacon* 12 September 1952. Letter Cadw to MLJR 30 December 1986. Cadw 1987. MBC listed building statistics.

84   Cadw 1987. Walker 1988. Bird 1991. Ward 1991.

85   Cadw 1987. *Beacon* 12 September 1952, 7 March 1986.

86   *News and Weekly Argus* 28 December 1989. *Beacon* 29 December 1989, 5 January 1990, 19 January 1990, 26 January 1990.

87   *Beacon* 29 March 1901, 30 July 1926.

88   *Beacon* 21 September 1934, 4 July 1941.

89   *Beacon* 3 July 1925, 9 October 1925.

90   *Beacon* 8 May 1931, 15 May 1931, 19 June 1931, 28 August 1931, 19 February 1937.

91   *Beacon* 28 March 1941, 30 May 1941, 27 June 1941. GCRO: C.R+B.M. 1940–2, 15 May 1941.
92   *Beacon* 11 July 1941, 8 August 1941.
93   *Beacon* 21 January 1944.
94   *Beacon* 21 May 1982.
95   *Beacon* 4 June 1982, 11 June 1982, 7 March 1986.
96   Welsh Office 1983 'Notes on Repair and Preservation of Masonry'. Ashurst and Ashurst 1988. Williams 1991.
97   *Beacon* 21 May 1982, 4 June 1982, 18 June 1982, 25 June 1982.
98   *Beacon* 4 October 1985, 22 November 1985.
99   *News and Weekly Argus* 23 January 1986. *Beacon* 7 March 1986.
100   *Beacon* 13 December 1985.
101   *Beacon* 27 December 1985, 17 January 1986, 7 March 1986. *News and Weekly Argus* 6 March 1986.
102   *Beacon* 9 October 1925, 13 August 1926, 2 March 1928, 16 March 1928, 11 May 1928.
103   *Beacon* 2 March 1928, 11 September 1931, 15 July 1932, 29 July 1932, 16 September 1932.
104   *Beacon* 27 June 1941, 4 July 1941, 11 July 1941. GCRO: C.R+B.M. 1940–2 4 April 1941, 27 October 1941.
105   MDC 1981. Monnow Bridge traffic figures for 20–6 July 1987 courtesy of GCCCES.
106   *Beacon* 4 October 1985, 14 February 1986, 21 March 1986.
107   MDC 1981. *Beacon* 25 July 1986. *News and Weekly Argus* 5 October 1989, 23 November 1989. Letter MBC to MLJR 22 May 1990.
108   *Beacon* 5 December 1986, 12 December 1986, 6 March 1987, 24 April 1987.
109   *Beacon* 7 August 1987, 13 November 1987, 27 November 1987, 11 December 1987, 18 December 1987, 11 November 1988, 23 December 1988, 7 April 1989, 28 July 1989, 3 November 1989, 10 November 1989. *South Wales Argus* 4 November 1987, 9 December 1987, 28 September 1989. *Western Mail* 24 December 1987, 8 November 1988. *Country Life* 28 January 1988. *The Guardian* 28 March 1989.
110   *Beacon* 8 December 1989, 19 January 1990, 15 March 1991, 12 April 1991, 28 June 1991, 19 July 1991, 18 October 1991, 29 November 1991, 21 February 1992, 18 June 1992, 10 December 1992, 4 February 1993, 14 October 1993, 11 November 1993. *Monmouth and Abergavenny News* 22 August 1991.
111   *Beacon* 10 April 1942, 24 April 1942.
112   One of the certificates, presented to C.A. Ferneyhough of the Royal Engineers, is at Monmouth Museum.
113   *Beacon* 27 September 1991, 29 November 1991, 15 April 1993, 30 September 1993.
114   Monmouth Museum: Minutes of Monmouth and District Chamber of Commerce meeting 27 June 1950, 25 March 1952. *Beacon* 5 March 1937.
115   Murray 1983.
116   Bagnall-Oakeley 1903, Jervoise 1936, Taylor 1951, Hando 1964, Richards 1984, and Barber 1989. Also see Brangwyn and Sparrow 1925, Toy 1939, Robins 1947, Smith 1953, de Maré 1954, Casson 1963, de Maré 1975, Davies 1978, Timpson 1989.
117   Andrews 1980. Pine 1984, 1986. *Beacon* 23 August 1991.
118   *Beacon* 23 March 1990, 7 December 1990. Clarke 1989. Kissack 1974, 1986, 1989. MAS 1989, 1991a. Monmouth Association 1988.
       On 13 May 1886 (*Beacon* 15 May 1886) water rose to within three inches of the top of the counter of Mr Higgins's shop at Overmonnow (Fig. 44).

119   Clayton 1933.

120   WWA 1984.

121   WWA 1984.

122   Tell-tales attached on 23 September 1988. Piling vibration tests on 9 October 1988. See also *News and Weekly Argus* 3 November 1988. *Beacon* 4 November 1988.

        In September 1989 the Welsh Water Authority divided. Part became Welsh Water PLC. The rest became part of the National Rivers Authority. The NRA assumed responsibility for the flood scheme.

123   Original plan and specifications for bed protection works in SWHP/WWA drawing MFS 134 dated March 1986.

124   The initial exploratory dig at the tower pier by SWHP/McAlpine occurred with GGAT, MAS, and MLJR observing. A second brief examination, with officials present, led to modification of the concrete bed design. See also *Beacon* 25 November 1988.

125   Rigold 1975, 1976. GGAT press release 1 November 1988. *South Wales Argus* 2 and 4 November 1988. *Beacon* 4 November 1988. *Western Mail* 9 November 1988.

126   *South Wales Argus* 4 November 1988. *Western Mail* 9 and 10 November 1988. *New Civil Engineer* 10 November 1988. Maylan 1988.

        Both timber structures when complete were evidently of Rigold's Type II construction, i.e. each pier was an oak trestle with a basic sole plate supporting several vertical timbers with bracing. A timber plate over the verticals would have carried joists supporting the roadway. Though a little more complex, a bridge of similar construction crossed the Wye at Chepstow until 1815, and at Whitney-on-Wye a wooden trestled bridge is in use still (built in 1780 and reconstructed several times) (Jervoise 1936, Martin 1973, Rigold 1975, Rigold 1976, Waters 1980, Gorvett 1984).

127   Morgan dendro-dating report July 1989. *Beacon* 1 September 1989.

128   The archaeological finds not left *in situ* were deposited at Monmouth Museum. *Beacon* 15 February 1991.

129   *Beacon* 2 February 1990, 4 May 1990. *South Wales Argus* 6 February 1990.

130   GCRO: C.R+B.M. 1940-1942 19 September 1940. *Beacon* 23 September 1955, 25 June 1982, 28 February 1986, 20 April 1990, 22 June 1990, 16 April 1992.

131   The drawing is numbered SUR R1 PL/NO 1 F/1.

132   GCRO: C.R+B.M. 28 June 1956, 26 July 1956. *Beacon* 14 September 1956.

133   Chamber of Commerce minutes 23 July 1957 in Monmouth Museum. *Beacon* 19 July 1957, 26 July 1957, 27 September 1957, 15 November 1957.

134   The ancient drain remains are clearly visible in several old drawings and engravings. It is seen in the September 1955 photograph by H.W. Plummer at Monmouth Museum. It had been destroyed by the Eric Warrilow photograph taken on 3 May 1958, also at Monmouth Museum.

        Another noticeable change between these photographs is the loss of the three houses between the bridge and the Barley Mow public house. Early in 1957 the houses were demolished and replaced by a rendered brick wall, the land becoming a yard for the Barley Mow.

135   Chamber of Commerce minutes for 28 May 1963 at Monmouth Museum. *Beacon* 8 February 1980.

136   *Beacon* 24 November 1989, 25 May 1990, 22 June 1990, 20 July 1990.

137   *Beacon* 12 May 1978, 2 June 1978.

138   *Beacon* 16 November 1889, 30 September 1955. Davies 1991. Davies 1993.

139   *Beacon* 3 October 1986, 20 March 1987, 24 April 1987, 18 December 1987, 20 May 1988, 10 February 1989, 24 February 1989, 23 June 1989, 1 September 1989, 8 September 1989, 15 September 1989, 29 September 1989, 13 October 1989, 3 November 1989. *Western Mail* 24 December 1987. *South Wales Argus* 29 June 1988, 12 October 1989. *News and Weekly Argus (Monmouth News)* 12 October 1989.

       Monnow Bridge Gatehouse Condition Report, Gwent County Council, January 1989.

       Gwent County Council press release 'Monnow Bridge Gatehouse to get expert repairs', 25 August 1989.

       Road closure for measurements and inspection occurred on 3 September. Preparations proceeded, the bridge being closed again on 15 October. The works were completed on 11 November 1989.

140   *Beacon* 13 October 1989.

141   Timber treatment 27 October 1989, guaranteed for ten years.

142   *Beacon* 1 December 1989, 29 December 1989, 5 January 1990, 19 January 1990, 26 January 1990. *News and Weekly Argus (Monmouth News)* 28 December 1989. Ashurst and Ashurst 1988. English Heritage leaflet *Principles of Repair*, October 1989.

143   Essay on restoration and conservation: Pearman 1990.

144   From photographs we find that, including the four springing stones, the south-west road arch had

       23 voussoirs in *c.*1860
       24 voussoirs in *c.*1890
       24 voussoirs in 1914
       25 voussoirs in 1975
       25 voussoirs in 1981
       28 voussoirs after the 1982 repairs
       25 voussoirs after the 1989 repairs.

       Original springing stone dimensions (measured 27 October 1989) off a stone from the downstream side removed temporarily during the 1989 works, with 1989 arch stone dimensions (measured 28 January 1990 and 21 March 1992) in parentheses: total height 12 in. (10 in.), height at front above chamfer 9 in. (7¾ in.), total depth 15½ in. (15 in.), depth behind chamfer 11½ in. (11½ in.), rebate height 5½ in., rebate depth 2½ in.

145   Other than the Carter drawings, the arch jambs and chamfering can be seen in illustrations by J.M.W. Turner, S. Prout, and Henry Gastineau.

       Loss of the jambs below the south-west road arch may account for the poor bonding of the masonry below that arch. It may be when the jambs were removed that the column of blocks poorly bonded to the adjacent wall appeared.

146   Arch stone ties outlined by Stonewest Cox in the Monnow Bridge new arch detail south elevation drawing 38090/1, dated October 1989.

147   *Beacon* 1 December 1989, 29 December 1989, 5 January 1990, 19 January 1990, 26 January 1990. *News and Weekly Argus (Monmouth News)* 28 December 1989.

148   *Beacon* 20 April 1990, 22 June 1990, 25 October 1991, 16 April 1992.

149   Report on Trial Pit Investigation and WWA 1984.

       The plans, elevations, and sections of Figs. 54, 60, 61, 62, and 63 are based upon information drawn from measurement and rectified photographs made by the author between Oct. 1985 and Sept. 1988. In the sectional drawings, structures cut through by the section are drawn solid black.

150   Advice on stone and mortar types present courtesy of Dr K.A. Moseley.

151   Borehole core information from WWA 1984.

     Four boreholes were made into the two piers. The cores were extracted and analysed to determine pier composition. Two of the bores (H1 and H2) were horizontal, one into each pier on the north-eastern side. The other two bores (R1 and R2) were into the north-east and south-west sides of pier one (the tower pier) drilling west-south-west and north-east and raked downward at 45° and 42° angles respectively.

     The horizontal boreholes indicate that ashlar stonework extends to a depth of 0.35 m. The interior of the piers is composed of rubble and cement. In the written analysis this is described as very strong light-grey fine-grained micaceous sandstone and moderately weak cement.

152   R1 borehole levels from WWA 1984. Monnow Gate benchmark altitude from the Ordnance Survey. Other levels from measurements by SWHP, GGAT, and MLJR taken in October/November 1988 during the flood alleviation works.

153   Fitchen 1981 discusses in detail the technology of medieval centrings and the advantages of arch rings. Also in Viollet-le-Duc's dictionary of medieval architecture.

154   Gwilt 1867. de Maré 1954. Fitchen 1981.

155   Utility services under the footpaths of Monnow Bridge (as of 1986), mostly enclosed in pipes: British Gas – a disused pipe. British Telecom – cables enclosed in one steel and one earthenware duct. WWA – one 6 in. water-main. MBC – no drainage pipes. South Wales Electricity Board – two 11,000 volt cables and one 415/240 volt cable. Information supplied by the relevant authorities.

156   Information on these and other fortified bridge gates can be found in the following sources – Bouguennec 1992, Brangwyn and Sparrow 1925, de Maré 1954, Emerson and Gromort 1925, Grose 1773-1787, Home 1931, Jackson 1971, Richards 1984, Robins 1947, Ward 1935, and Whitney 1929.

157   Employing Sailhan's (1978) classification system, the plain loops are type Ia A 1, with a chamfered outer face to the loops and embrasures headed by stepped lintels.

158   The drawings and patent roll were removed to Monmouth Museum in 1985 and were later conserved.

159   Bagnall-Oakeley 1903.

160   *Beacon* 9 May 1902.

161   Hillman 1881, Waugh 187_, Waugh 1879.

162   Employing Sailhan's (1978) classification system, the cruciform loop is type IVb A 2, with round splayed oillets, a slightly sloping embrasure bed, and an embrasure head of stepped lintels.

References

Andrews, W. 1890. *Old-time Punishments*. London: William Andrews and Co.

Andrews, S.E. 1980. *Crested China – The History of Heraldic Souvenir Ware*. London: Springwood Books.

Anon. 1989. *Leeds Castle*. London: Philip Wilson.

Ashurst, J., and N. Ashurst. 1988. *Practical Building Conservation: English Heritage technical handbook. Stone Masonry*. Aldershot: Gower Technical Press.

Bagnall-Oakeley, M.E. 1896. 'The Fortifications of Monmouth'. *Proc. Monmouthshire and Caerleon Antiq. Assoc.*

Bagnall-Oakeley, M.E. 1903. *Monnow Bridge Tower*. Monmouthshire County Council.

Barber, C. (ed.). 1989. *Hando's Gwent. Volume Two*. Abergavenny: Blorenge Books.

Barley, M.W. 1975. 'Town Defences in England and Wales after 1066'. In M.W. Barley (ed.). *The Plans and Topography of Medieval Towns in England and Wales*. The Council for British Archaeology.

Beattie, W. 1842. *The Castles and Abbeys of England, from the National Records, Early Chronicles, and other Standard Authors*. London: J.S. Virtue and Co.

Bird, C. 1991. 'Statutory all-change'. *English Heritage Conservation Bulletin* 13:10–11.

Birbeck, T.T. 1973. *Sword and Ploughshare – The Story of the de Bohuns and Caldicot*. Chepstow: The Chepstow Society.

Bouguennec, R. 1992. *Ponts et Merveilles*. Landerneau, France: Carré Noir.

Bowen, J.A. 1982. 'Architectural Description' [of the West Gate, Canterbury]. In S.S. Frere, S. Stow, and P. Bennett. *Excavations on the Roman and Medieval Defences of Canterbury*. Maidstone: Kent Archaeological Society.

Bradney, J.A. 1907a. *A History of Monmouthshire from the coming of the Normans into Wales down to the present time*. London: Mitchell, Hughes, & Clarke.

Bradney, J.A. (ed.). 1907b. *The Diary of Walter Powell of Llantilio Crossenny in the County of Monmouth, Gentleman. 1603-1654*. Bristol: John Wright and Co.

Brangwyn, F., and W.S. Sparrow. 1925. *A Book of Bridges*. London: The Bodley Head.

Britton, J. and E.W. Brayley. 1801–15. *The Beauties of England and Wales; or, original delineations, topographical, historical, and descriptive, of each county*. London: Vernor, Hood, & Sharpe.

Cadw: Welsh Historic Monuments. 1987. *Schedule of Ancient Monuments of National Importance – Gwent*. Cardiff: Cadw: Welsh Historic Monuments.

Camden, W. 1735. *Britannia, or, A Chorographical Description of Great Britain and Ireland, Together with the Adjacent Islands*. London.

Casson, H. 1963. *Bridges*. London: Chatto & Windus Ltd.

Chatelain, A. 1987. *Châteaux forts – images de pierre des guerres médiévales*. Paris: Rempart.

Clarke, S. 1987a. 'Recent Discoveries in Monmouth, Gwent.' *Archaeology in Wales* 27:30–1.

Clarke, S. 1987b. 'Burton Homes, Glendower Street (SO5088 1270).' *Archaeology in Wales* 27:61.

Clarke, S. 1989. 'Monmouth.' *Current Archaeology* 10:254–7.

Clayton, C.H.J. 1933. *General Report on the 'Main River' Wye*. River Wye Catchment Board.

Colvin, H.M. (ed.). 1963. *The History of the King's Works*. London: HMSO.

Cotman, J.S. 1838. *Liber Studiorum*. London: Henry Bohn.

The Marquis Curzon of Kedleston, KG. 1926. *Bodiam Castle, Sussex. A Historical & Descriptive Survey*. London: Jonathan Cape.

Davies, E.T. 1978. *A Guide to the Castles of Gwent*. Newport, Gwent: R.H. Johns Ltd.

Davies, P. 1991. '"Improvements" in Historic Areas'. *English Heritage Conservation Bulletin* 15:15–16.

Davies, P. 1993. 'Street Improvement in Historic Areas'. *English Heritage Conservation Bulletin* 21: 8–9.

de Maré, E. 1954. *Bridges of Britain*. London: B.T. Batsford.

de Maré, E. 1975. *Bridges of Britain*. London: B.T. Batsford.

Emerson, W., and G. Gromort. 1925. *Old Bridges of France*. New York: American Institute of Architects.

Fitchen, J. 1981. *The Construction of Gothic Cathedrals – A Study of Medieval Vault Erection*. London: University of Chicago Press.

Gilpin, W. 1782. *Observations on the River Wye, and several parts of South Wales, &c. relative chiefly to Picturesque Beauty; made in the Summer of the Year 1770, By William Gilpin, M.A. Vicar of Boldre near Lymington*. London: R. Blamire.

Glamorgan-Gwent Archaeological Trust. 1987. '83-85 Monnow Street, Monmouth (SO 506 127).' *GGAT Annual Review* 10-13.

Gorvett, D. 1984. *Bridge over the River Wye*. R. and A.S. Broadhurst.

Grose, F. 1773-87. *The Antiquities of England and Wales*. London: Hooper & Wigstead.

Gwilt, J. 1867. *The Encyclopedia of Architecture – Historical, Theoretical, and Practical*. London: Longmans.

Hando, F.J. 1964. *Monmouth Town Sketch Book*. Newport, Gwent: R.H. Johns Ltd.

Hardy, T.D. (ed.). 1833. *Rotuli Litterarum Clausarum*. Vol. I. London: Record Commissioners.

Harris, E. 1910. *History of Cooling Castle*. Rochester: Edwin Harris & Sons.

Harris, J. 1719. *The History of Kent*. London.

Hearne, T. (ed.). 1769. *The Itinerary of John Leland the Antiquary*. Oxford: Thomas Hearne.

Heath, C. 1804. *Historical and Descriptive Accounts of the Ancient and Present State of the Town of Monmouth, including a Variety of Particulars deserving the Stranger's Notice, relating to the Borough and its Neighbourhood*. Monmouth: Charles Heath.

Heath, C. 1808. *The Excursion Down the Wye*. Monmouth: Charles Heath.

Heath, C. 1818. *Extracts from the Act of Parliament for Paving the Footways, and Cleansing, Lighting, and Watching, the Streets, in the Town of Monmouth*. Monmouth: Charles Heath.

Hewlett, H.G. (ed.). 1886–9. *The Flowers of History by Roger de Wendover*. London: HMSO.

Hillman, S. 1881. *Hillman's Illustrated Historical Handbook for Tourists to Chepstow, Windcliff, Tintern Abbey, Monmouth, Raglan, the Castles and Ancient Remains of Wentwood, and other Places of Interest on and about the Wye*. Chepstow: Alfred Hillman.

Home, G. 1931. *Old London Bridge*. London: The Bodley Head.

Jackson, P. 1971. *London Bridge*. London: Cassell and Co. Ltd.

James, T. 1980. *Carmarthen: An Archaeological and Topographical Survey*. Carmarthen: Carmarthenshire Antiq. Soc.

Jervoise, E. 1936. *The Ancient Bridges of Wales and Western England*. London: The Architectural Press.

Johns, C.N. 1978. *Caerphilly Castle*. Cardiff: HMSO.

Jones, P.N., and D. Renn. 1982. 'The military effectiveness of Arrow Loops – Some experiments at White Castle'. *Chateau Gaillard* 9–10:445–56.

Kenyon, J.R. 1986. *Kidwelly Castle*. Cardiff: Cadw: Welsh Historic Monuments.

Kenyon, J.R. 1990. *Medieval Fortifications*. Leicester: Leicester University Press.

King, D.J.C. 1988. *The Castle in England and Wales – An Interpretative History*. Beckenham: Croom Helm.

Kissack, K.E. 1974. *Mediaeval Monmouth*. Monmouth: Monmouth Historical and Educational Trust.

Kissack, K.E. 1986. *Victorian Monmouth*. Monmouth: Monmouth Historical and Educational Trust.

Kissack, K.E. 1989. *The Building of Monmouth*. Monmouth: Monmouth Historical and Educational Trust.

Kissack, K.E. 1991. 'Life in the Monmouth Militia: 1778 to 1812'. *The Monmouthshire Antiquary* 7:71–81.

Knight, J.K. 1977. 'Usk Castle and its Affinities'. In M.R. Apted, R. Gilyard-Beer, and A.D. Saunders (eds.). *Ancient Monuments and their Interpretation*. London: Phillimore and Co.

Knight, J.K. 1986. *Chepstow Castle*. Cardiff: Cadw: Welsh Historic Monuments.

Knight, J.K. 1992. *The Three Castles*. Cardiff: Cadw: Welsh Historic Monuments.

Luard, H.R. (ed.). 1876. *Matthaei Parisiensis, Monachi Sancti Albani, Chronica Majora*. London: Longman and Co.

Martin, D. 1973. 'Bodiam Castle Medieval Bridges'. *Hastings Area Archaeological Papers* No. 1.

Maylan, C.N. 1988. 'Monmouth (SO 5043 1251)'. *Archaeology in Wales* 28:73.

Miles, A.H. (ed.). 1898. *The Poets and the Poetry of the Century*. London: Hutchinson and Co.

Monmouth, County of. 1844. *General Rules for Regulating the Practice of the Court of General Quarter Sessions of the Peace, and other Matters relating to the General Police and Affairs of the County of Monmouth, originally established by Order of the Court, at the Easter Quarter Sessions, 1836*. Usk: J.H. Clark.

Monmouth, County of. 1857. *General Rules for Regulating the Practice of the Court of General Quarter Sessions of the Peace, and other Proceedings relating to the General Affairs of the County, established by Order of the Court*. Newport: M. Evans.

Monmouth Archaeological Society. 1989. *Discoveries in Monnow Street Monmouth*. Monmouth: Monmouth Arch. Soc.

Monmouth Archaeological Society. 1991a. *22–24 Monnow Street and other work on Roman and Medieval Monmouth during 1990–91*. Monmouth: Monmouth Arch. Soc.

Monmouth Archaeological Society. 1991b. *Recent Archaeological Work in Monmouth*. Monmouth: Monmouth Arch. Soc. Reprinted from *Archaeology in Wales*.

Monmouth Association. 1988. 'The Hundred Year Flood.' *Newsletter of the Monmouth Association* 2.

Monmouth District Council. 1981. *Monmouth Town Centre Plan Review*. Mamhilad, Gwent: Monmouth District Council.

Moore, A.W. 1982. *John Sell Cotman 1782–1842*. Norwich: Norfolk Museums Service.

Morton, C. 1981. *Bodiam Castle*. London: The National Trust.

Moss, F. 1903. *Pilgrimages to Old Homes mostly on the Welsh Border*. Didsbury: F. Moss.

Murray, R.H. 1983. *Dinmore Manor and the Commandery of the Knights Hospitaller of St. John of Jerusalem at Dinmore, Herefordshire*. Dinmore, Herefordshire: G.H. Murray.

National Trust. 1992. *Scotney Castle*. London: The National Trust.

Newman, J. 1976. *West Kent and the Weald*. In N. Pevsner (ed.). *The Buildings of England*. Harmondsworth: Penguin Books.

Nichols, W.N. 1979. *Cooling (Kent) and its Castle*. Redhill, Surrey: W.N. Nichols.

O'Neill, B.H. St.J. 1960. *Castles and Cannon*. Oxford: Clarendon Press.

Pearman, H. 1990. 'If the façade fits . . . what price authentic restoration?' *The Sunday Times* 21 January 1990.

Peers, C. 1982. *Carisbrooke Castle*. London: HMSO.

Perks, J.C. 1967. *Chepstow Castle*. London: HMSO.

Phillips, J.R. 1874. *Memoirs of the Civil War in Wales and the Marches*. London: Longmans, Green, and Co.

Pine, N.J. 1984. *Goss and Other Crested China*. Aylesbury: Shire Publications Ltd.

Pine, N.J. 1986. *The 1986 Price Guide to Goss China*. Horndean, Hampshire: Milestone Publications.

Prout, S. 1813-14. *Rudiments of Landscape: in Progressive Studies. Drawn and Etched in Imitation of Chalk, by Samuel Prout*. London: R. Ackermann.

Radford, C.A.R. 1952. *Kidwelly Castle*. London: HMSO.

Radford, C.A.R. 1980. *Llawhaden Castle*. London: HMSO.

Radford, C.A.R. 1982. *White Castle*. Cardiff: HMSO.

Rajnai, M., and M. Allthorpe-Guyton. 1979. *John Sell Cotman 1782–1842. Early Drawings (1798–1812) in Norwich Castle Museum*. Norwich: Norfolk Museums Service.

Reid, C. 1983. *St. Donat's Castle*. Llantwit Major: Atlantic College.

Rees, W. (ed.). 1953. *A Survey of the Duchy of Lancaster Lordships in Wales – 1609–1613*. Cardiff: University of Wales Press.

Renn, D.F. 1981. 'Tonbridge and Some Other Gatehouses'. In A. Detsicas (ed.). *Collectanea Historica – Essays in Memory of Stuart Rigold*. Maidstone: Kent Archaeological Society.

Renn, D.F. 1982. 'A Note on the West Gate Gunloops'. In S.S. Frere, S. Stow, and P. Bennett. *Excavations on the Roman and Medieval Defences of Canterbury*. Maidstone: Kent Archaeological Society.

Renn, D.F. 1989. *Caerphilly Castle*. Cardiff: Cadw: Welsh Historic Monuments.

Richards, J.M. 1984. *The National Trust Book of Bridges*. London: Jonathan Cape.

Rigold, S.E. 1975. 'Structural Aspects of Medieval Timber Bridges.' *Medieval Archaeology* 19:48–91.

Rigold, S.E. 1976. 'Structural Aspects of Medieval Timber Bridges: Addenda.' *Medieval Archaeology* 20:152–3.

Robins, F.W. 1947. *The Story of the Bridge*. Birmingham: Cornish Bros.

Round, J.H. 1899. *Calendar of Documents Preserved in France*. London: HMSO.

Sailhan, P. 1978. 'Typologie des archeres et canonnieres.' *Bull. Soc. Antiq. Ouest* 14:511–41.

Shoesmith, R. 1990. 'Excavations in Monmouth, 1973'. *The Monmouthshire Antiquary* 6:1–15.

Smith, H.S. 1953. *The World's Great Bridges*. London: Phoenix House Ltd.

Smith, L.T. 1964. *The Itinerary of John Leland in or about the years 1536–9*. London: Centaur Press.

Speed, J. 1610. *The Theatre of the Empire of Great Britain*. London: Sudbury & Humble.

Taylor, A.J. 1951. *Monmouth Castle and Great Castle House*. London: HMSO.

Thompson, M.W. 1977. *Kenilworth Castle*. London: HMSO.

Thompson, M.W. 1991. *Kenilworth Castle*. London: English Heritage.

Timpson, J. 1989. *Timpson's Towns of England and Wales – Oddities and Curiosities*. Norwich: Jarrold Colour Publications.

Toy, S. 1939. *Castles – A Short History of Fortification from 1600 B.C. to A.D. 1600*. London: W. Heinemann.

Turner, H.L. 1971. *Town Defences in England and Wales*. London: John Baker.

Viollet-le-Duc, E.E. 1854–68. *Dictionnaire raisonné de L'Architecture Francaise du XIe au XVIe siecle*. Paris: A. Morel.

Walker, R. 1988. *The Cambridgeshire Guide to Historic Buildings Law*. Cambridge: Cambridgeshire County Council.

Ward, A. 1991. 'The Listing of Historic Buildings'. In J. Bold (ed.). *Recording Historic Buildings*. London: Royal Commission on the Historical Monuments of England.

Ward, A.W. 1935. *The Bridges of Shrewsbury*. Shrewsbury: Wilding & Son.

Waters, I. 1980. *Chepstow Road Bridges*. Chepstow: Ivor Waters.

Watson, P. 1984. *A Short History of Hever Castle*. Tunbridge Wells: P. Watson.

Waugh, R. 187_. *Illustrated Handbook to Monmouth and the various Objects of Interest in and around it. New and Enlarged Edition*. Monmouth: R. Waugh.

Waugh, R. 1879. *Illustrated Handbook to Monmouth and the various Objects of Interest in and around it. Fourth Thousand*. Monmouth: R. Waugh.

Webb, J., and T.W. Webb. 1879. *Memorials of the Civil War between King Charles I and the Parliament of England as it affected Herefordshire and the Adjacent Counties*. London: Longmans, Green, and Co.

Welsh Water Authority. 1984. *Monmouth Flood Alleviation Scheme – Stability of Monnow Bridge Final Report*.

Whitney, C.S. 1929. *Bridges – A Study in their Art, Science and Evolution*. New York: W.E. Rudge.

Williams, G.B.A. 1991. *Pointing stone and brick walling*. London: Society for the Protection of Ancient Buildings.

Wykeham-Martin, C. 1869. *The History and Description of Leeds Castle, Kent*. Westminster: Nichols & Sons.

Acknowledgements

Without the assistance of many people and institutions production of this book would not have been possible.

For access to the collections of Monmouth Museum and the Monmouth Borough Archives I am indebted to A. Helme.

Regarding the Monmouth flood alleviation scheme at Monnow Bridge I am grateful to C.D. James (SWHP) for information, time, and site access.

I am grateful also for information and advice from the following – R. Bouguennec, British Gas, British Telecom, Cadw: Welsh Historic Monuments, Gwent County Council, D.J.C. King, K.E. Kissack, J.K. Knight, C.N. Maylan (GGAT), Monmouth Borough Council, J.G. Morgan (GCCCES), R.K. Morris, K.A. Moseley, South Wales Electricity, A.J. Taylor, and the Welsh Water Authority.

I am grateful to the owners/guardians of the following sites who allowed access for the examination of features and access to parts not normally accessible: Benton Castle, Cooling Castle, Hever Castle, Kenilworth Castle, Leybourne Castle, Rye Land Gate, Tonbridge Castle, and Usk Castle.

I thank the following for permission to reproduce illustrations in this guide (figure number and illustration reference in parentheses): His Grace the Duke of Beaufort (Fig. 6), Birmingham Museums and Art Gallery (Fig. 9), the British Library (Fig. 17, ADD.29938 f.11 f.12 f.13), the Tate Gallery (Fig. 16, TBXXVI-63), Mrs Michael T. Harding-Rolls and Gwent County Record Office (Fig. 22, D361 F/P Misc 1), Monmouth Museum (Figs. 5, 7, 8, 11, 20, 30, 32, 33, 34, 35, 37, 38, 43, 44, 45, 73), the National Library of Wales (Fig. 14, NLW PD5692), the National Museum of Wales (Fig. 23, 15.238), the Public Record Office and the Controller of Her Majesty's Stationery Office (Fig. 1, C66/117 pt.2 m.6), the Royal Commission on Ancient and Historical Monuments in Wales (Fig. 29, BB72/4360), and the owner of Fig. 10.

Detail of J.S. Cotman's soft ground etching of Monnow Bridge viewed from the east, published as plate 26 in his *Liber Studiorum*.